THE AMAZING COLLECTION™

PAUL'S LETTERS TO PASTORS

Wellspring for Life
Song

"Precious Lord"
Kristi Walker

SET 10

THE
AMAZING
COLLECTION™

Paul's Letters to Pastors

1 Timothy, 2 Timothy,
Titus, and Philemon

Set 10

BIG
DREAM
MINISTRIES

No part of *The Amazing Collection*, whether audio, video, or print, may be reproduced in any form without written permission from Big Dream Ministries, Inc., P.O. Box 324, 12460 Crabapple Road, Suite 202, Alpharetta, Georgia 30004. 1-678-366-3460
www.theamazingcollection.org

ISBN-13: 978-1-932199-10-9
ISBN-10: 1-932199-10-1

Cover design by Brand Navigation and Arvid Wallen
Cover composite image by Getty Images and Corbis
Creative Team: Leigh McLeroy, Kathy Mosier, Pat Reinheimer

Some of the anecdotal illustrations in this book are true to life and are included with the permission of the persons involved. All other illustrations are composites of real situations, and any resemblance to people living or dead is coincidental.

Unless otherwise identified, all Scripture quotations in this publication are taken from the *New American Standard Bible* (NASB), © The Lockman Foundation 1960, 1962, 1963, 1968, 1971, 1972, 1973, 1975, 1977, 1995. Other versions used include *The Living Bible* (TLB), Copyright © 1971, used by permission of Tyndale House Publishers, Inc., Wheaton, IL 60189, all rights reserved and the HOLY BIBLE: NEW INTERNATIONAL VERSION® (NIV®), Copyright © 1973, 1978, 1984 by International Bible Society, used by permission of Zondervan Publishing House, all rights reserved.

Printed in the United States

6 7 8 9 10 / 18 17 16 15 14

Welcome to
The Amazing Collection
The Bible, Book by Book

It is amazing how a love letter arriving at just the right time can gladden the heart, refresh the soul, and restore the passion of the beloved. When lovers are separated by distance and can communicate only through the written word, that word becomes the lifeline of their love.

The greatest love letter ever written often sits on our shelves unopened as we go about our lives, sometimes fearful, burdened, anxious, in pain, and in doubt, not knowing that on its pages we can find all we need to live the life we have always wanted.

In this love letter we will discover God, and through Him we will receive hope, assurance, freedom from fear, guidance for everyday life, wisdom, joy, peace, power, and above all, the way to salvation. We will find the life we have always longed for — *abundant* life.

The Bible is simply a love letter compiled into sixty-six books and written over a period of sixteen hundred years by more than forty authors living on three continents. Although the authors came from different backgrounds, there is one message, one theme, one thread that runs throughout the entire Bible from the first book, Genesis, to the last book, Revelation. That message is God's redeeming love for mankind — a message that is as relevant for us today as it was two thousand years ago.

God has written the Bible so that men and women might enter into an intimate relationship with Him and see His character, His works, His power, and His love. It would be tragic to read these books and never come to know your God! Therefore, as you go through this study, listen to the lectures, read the Scripture, and do your daily homework. Make it your heart's desire to know God intimately. Read each page of the Bible as if it were a love letter written by the hand of God to you personally. Bask in His great love, stand in awe of His mighty power, bow before His majesty, and give thanksgiving and adoration to the One who is all-present, all-knowing, all-merciful, and all-loving. He is on every page, and He is speaking to you.

The Bible is a book inspired by God Himself. It is His story, His love letter, His invitation to you to become His child through His Son, Jesus Christ. It is the Word of God . . . indeed, the most Amazing Collection.

CONTENTS

MAPS, CHARTS, AND DIAGRAMS

WORKBOOK GUIDE

The Amazing Collection is a study of the Bible, book by book. This tenth study focuses on the letters Paul wrote to three pastors of the early church. The following will acquaint you with the design of this series.

The entire Bible will be studied one book at a time through a teaching video and a written study. The teaching video includes music to stir the heart, graphics to enlighten the mind, and a personal testimony to bring the theme of that particular book to life.

The workbook contains:

1. An introduction to summarize each book.

2. Outlines to be used while watching each of the teaching videos. The answers to the outline blanks are given during the videos and can also be found in the key at the back of your workbook.

3. *Learning for Life* discussion questions to be used after viewing the videos. (If your group is large, we recommend forming small discussion groups.)

4. Five daily lessons of homework for each book.

5. A memory verse for each book.

6. Various maps, charts, and diagrams.

7. A review at the end of each book to refresh your memory. The answers to the review are found in the *Review It!* sections in the margins at the end of the lessons for Day One through Day Four. The fifth review question is a review of the memory verse.

Before you begin the homework, ask God to show you how to apply the truths of Scripture to your own life. At the beginning of each day's lesson in the workbook, there are two choices for the daily reading. The *Complete Read* enables you to read the entire book over the course of that study. During busy times, the *Quick Read* allows you to read a few key chapters or verses from that book. The daily lesson will require a small amount of time each day to complete. Of course, feel free to extend that time with additional study.

One of the incredible things about the Word of God is that you can read the same Scripture at different times in your life and gain new insights with each reading. God's Word is inexhaustible, and it is living; it has the power to produce life-changing results.

Our prayer for you as you journey through *The Amazing Collection* is that you will learn for life the purpose, main character, geography, and time period of every book in the Bible. But above all, we pray that you will come to know more intimately the God of the Bible, His Son Jesus Christ, and the Holy Spirit.

PAUL'S LETTERS TO PASTORS AT A GLANCE

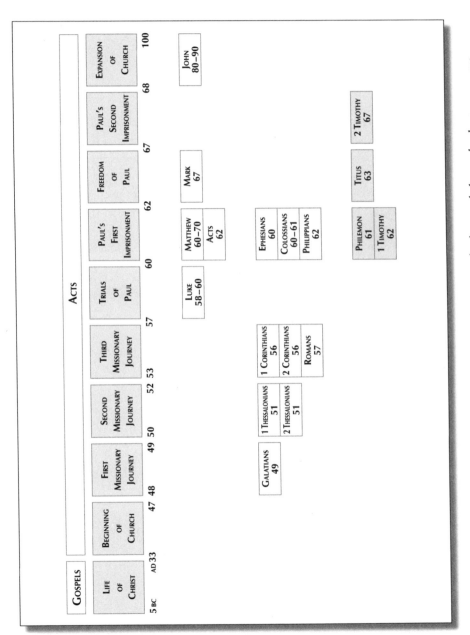

To see how these books fit into the chronology of the New Testament books as a whole, see the chart on page 119.

Overview of

PAUL'S LETTERS TO PASTORS

The following pages provide an overview of each of the books you will be studying in this set. They are designed to be cut out and used as quick reference cards with the main facts of the book on the front and the memory verse on the back.

You might find it helpful to laminate them and carry them with you on a ring or keep them in a card holder in a place where you'll be able to refer to them often.

It is our hope that this will be a tool that will help you truly learn these books for life.

I TIMOTHY
Instructions on Leadership

WHO:

Paul

Timothy

WHAT:

A Personal Letter About the Role of a Pastor

WHERE:

From Philippi

To Timothy in Ephesus

Time Written: AD 62

---

2 TIMOTHY
Instructions on Endurance

WHO:

Paul

Timothy

WHAT:

Timothy's Commissioning Letter and Combat Manual for Endurance

WHERE:

From Prison in Rome

To Timothy in Ephesus

Time Written: AD 67

TITUS
Instructions on Church Order

WHO:

Paul

Titus

WHAT:

A Letter of Instruction to the Church and Its Leaders

WHERE:

From Paul, Perhaps in Corinth

To Titus on the Mediterranean Island of Crete

Time Written: AD 63

1 TIMOTHY
Instructions on Leadership

*I write so that you will know how one ought to
conduct himself in the household of God,
which is the church of the living God.*

1 TIMOTHY 3:15

2 TIMOTHY
Instructions on Endurance

*You therefore, my son,
be strong in the grace that is in Christ Jesus.*

2 TIMOTHY 2:1

TITUS
Instructions on Church Order

*Speak confidently, so that those who have believed God
will be careful to engage in good deeds.*

TITUS 3:8

PHILEMON
Instructions on Forgiveness

WHO:

Paul

Philemon

Onesimus

WHAT:

A Letter to Philemon
Regarding the
Forgiveness of His
Runaway Slave,
Onesimus

WHERE:

From Prison in Rome

To Philemon in
Colossae

Time Written: AD 61

PHILEMON
Instructions on Forgiveness

If then you regard me a partner, accept him as you would me.

PHILEMON 17

INTRODUCTION TO
PAUL'S LETTERS TO PASTORS

The previous nine letters of the apostle Paul were written to local churches in the first century AD. The next four letters were written to individual men responsible for leadership in three different churches: Timothy in Ephesus, Titus on the island of Crete, and Philemon in Colossae. These letters were written over a period of six years, from AD 61 to 67. Second Timothy is Paul's last epistle penned from prison, most likely just months before his martyrdom.

From the very beginning of the church, leadership was necessary, and appropriate leaders and their leadership roles had to be established. Thus, as you study these books, you will become acquainted with the character traits of a leader, the various forms of leadership, the descriptions of ministry for various groups of people within the church, and the warnings against false teachers and practices.

All of this was new ground in the first century AD, and under the guidance of the Holy Spirit, it was ground broken well and permanently. Two millennia later, biblical churches still look to these books for direction in the area of church leadership.

I TIMOTHY

[Instructions on Leadership]

I write so that you will know how one ought to

conduct himself in the household of God,

which is the church of the living God.

1 TIMOTHY 3:15

I Timothy
[Instructions on Leadership]

INTRODUCTION

Paul's first letter to Timothy is the first of four New Testament letters written by the apostle to men serving in positions of pastoral leadership in the early church. These letters differ greatly from the first nine Pauline Epistles, all written to churches. Here Paul focuses much more specifically on church structure and ground rules.

It could not have been easy for the recipients of Paul's instruction to assume and carry out positions of leadership in the first-century church. Everything was new. Everything came under scrutiny. Everything was countercultural. Realizing these men's needs and their inexperience, the apostle Paul, under the inspiration of the Holy Spirit, laid down guidelines for order and stability that are striking in their genius, wisdom, and practicality.

The book of I Timothy is the strongest and most complete of the four Pastoral Epistles. Under its guidance, a called and gifted leader of God in any century could begin a local church, assured of laying a foundation that would be right and sufficient for vital, long-term ministry.

Much of what you read may already be familiar to you, and you might think it is common knowledge. But try to imagine receiving all this instruction at a time when none of it had ever been done before.

I Timothy
[Instructions on Leadership]

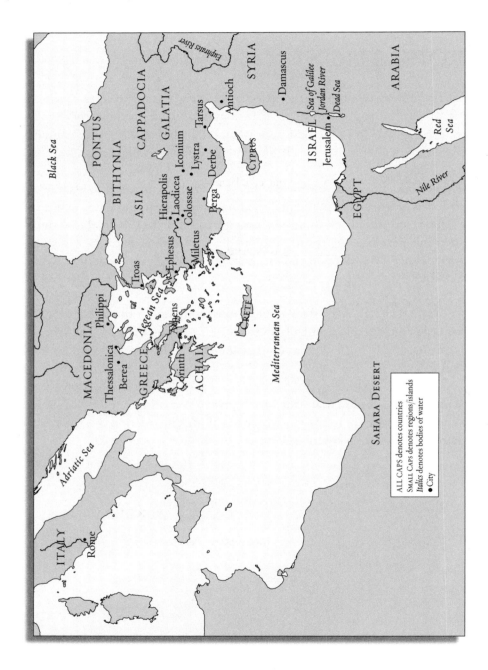

I Timothy
[Instructions on Leadership]

OVERVIEW

WHO: Author: Paul
Main Character: Timothy

WHAT: A personal letter about the role of a pastor

WHEN: AD 62

WHERE: Written from Philippi to Timothy in Ephesus

WHY: To provide guidance for the proper conduct of leadership within the church

I. **PAUL'S INSTRUCTION CONCERNING DOCTRINE (I TIMOTHY 1)**

  A. The ___Goal___ of sound doctrine is:

   1. ___Love___ from a pure heart

   2. So one might keep a clean ___Conscience___

   3. So believers will increase in a sincere ___Faith___

  B. Paul ___defended___ sound doctrine.

   1. Avoid ___Legalism___.

   2. Avoid ___Gnosticism___ (No Resurrection)

  C. Paul testified to God's ___Grace___.

  D. Paul instructed Timothy to "___Fight the good fight___" (I Timothy 1:18).

II. **PAUL'S INSTRUCTION CONCERNING PUBLIC WORSHIP (I TIMOTHY 2)**

  A. ___Prayer___ is the most essential part of public worship.

  B. Prayer includes:

   1. ___Entreaties___ (desires, needs)

   2. ___Prayers___ (bold access to God)

3. _Petitions_ (requests, intercessions)

4. _Thanksgiving_ (giving thanks)

C. Paul gave instruction for women in the church.

  1. They must _dress_ properly.

III. PAUL'S INSTRUCTION CONCERNING CHURCH LEADERS (1 TIMOTHY 3)

A. Paul listed the character traits of an _elder_ (bishop).

  1. His job is to oversee the _spiritual_ life of the church.

  2. He must be above _reproach_.

  3. He must be tolerant, prudent, respectful, hospitable, and able to _teach_.

  4. He must have a good _reputation_ outside of the church.

B. Paul listed the character traits of a _deacon_.

  1. The traits of a deacon are similar to that of an _elder_.

  2. The deacon's job is to _serve_.

IV. PAUL'S INSTRUCTION CONCERNING FALSE TEACHERS (1 TIMOTHY 4)

A. Paul _identified_ the false teachers.

B. He instructed Timothy to _stand_ firm against false teachers:

  1. _Know_ the Word of God.

  2. _Discipline_ yourself for godliness.

  3. _Fix_ your hope on the living God.

  4. Read, teach, and _exhort_ through the Word of God.

  5. _Use_ your spiritual gifts.

  6. _Persevere_ in these things.

V. PAUL'S INSTRUCTION CONCERNING PASTORS' RELATIONSHIPS WITH CHURCH MEMBERS (1 TIMOTHY 5:1–6:5)

A. Treat all with _____respect_____ and honor them as family.

B. _____Widows_____ have a special place in the church.

C. _____Honor_____ godly elders and discipline those who continue in sin.

D. False teachers should be _____identified_____.

VI. PAUL'S INSTRUCTION CONCERNING TIMOTHY (1 TIMOTHY 6:6-21)

A. Flee from the love of _____money_____.

B. _____Fight_____ the good fight.

APPLICATION

You are in a battle with the world, with Satan, and with your old sin nature — and the battle is for your heart and soul. Fight the good fight!

I TIMOTHY
[Instructions on Leadership]

LEARNING FOR LIFE

1. In 1 Timothy 1:5, Paul describes the three goals of his instruction. Review them and explain what these goals would look like in a Christian today. Do you know someone who radiates these characteristics? Which one of these areas do you feel you need help with?

2. Describe the fight that Timothy was in. What weapons did he need to fight the good fight?

3. Why should prayer be an integral part of the church gathering together?

4. List the character qualities an elder must have. Why do you think each one of these is important for the role of eldership?

5. Read 1 Timothy 4:7-8. What would be involved in disciplining oneself for godliness? As a leader in the church, why would this be so important?

[Handwritten annotations:]

Love from a pure heart
good conscience
sincere faith

there's faith
in prayer

Christ
False doctrine —

It's how we communicate w/Him

above reproach — Tolerant
Prudent, respectful, hospitable — able to teach — good rep —

- Be in the Word —
Know the Work of God
Discipline ourselves
Obey Him

Book
The Invisible War

Focus - Fix your eyes on the living God —

make Him your all in all !

I TIMOTHY
[Instructions on Leadership]

DAY ONE

COMPLETE READ: Chapters 1–6

QUICK READ: Chapters 1–6

THE BIG PICTURE

First Timothy introduces a short section of books written by Paul to pastors, and Timothy could surely use the apostle's instruction and encouragement. Timothy was young; he could benefit from instruction from an older man. Timothy was inexperienced; he could use counsel from someone further down the road. Timothy was hard-pressed; he could be encouraged by a mentor's stirring boldness.

As a leader in the church at Ephesus, Timothy carried the mantle of responsibility for many areas: opposing false doctrine; blending that opposition with love and sensitivity; teaching his flock to live a life of righteousness; ensuring that the elders were men of character; providing care for widows; safeguarding worship and the public reading of the Scriptures; establishing his leadership in the midst of older folks; and pursuing personal righteousness, faith, love, perseverance, and gentleness.

This was a tall order for a young, inexperienced, and timid man. But Paul had confidence in Timothy and placed himself in the role of mentor to his up-and-coming protégé.

Following his release from his first imprisonment in Rome, Paul journeyed to the city of Ephesus and to other Asian cities. Timothy came from Philippi to join him in Ephesus. When Paul decided to move on, he left Timothy in Ephesus (1 Timothy 1:3) to pastor and protect the church that had been established in that city about a decade earlier. Paul undoubtedly realized the

DID YOU KNOW?
The books of 1 and 2 Timothy, Titus, and Philemon became known as the Pastoral Epistles during the eighteenth century.

One other thing stirs me when I look back at my youthful days, the fact that so many people gave me something or were something to me without knowing it.
—ALBERT SCHWEITZER, French missionary, philosopher, and physician

tremendous responsibility he had laid at his young friend's feet, so he soon sat down and wrote to him what has become known as 1 Timothy. It was most likely written from the city of Philippi in or around AD 62.

In this first letter to Timothy (a second would follow about five years later), Paul laid out what was essentially a leadership manual for the local church. Second Timothy and Titus will expand this manual, but the great majority of leadership principles and practices are described here. Thus our theme: leadership of a local church.

Because the content of the letter is so broad and diverse and the style so conversational and personal, it is difficult to discern a natural outline for the letter. One way to view the material looks like this:

Leadership of a Local Church Concerning:					
Sound Doctrine	Public Worship	Church Leaders	False Teachers	Church Members	Timothy Himself
Key Verse: 1:3	Key Verse: 2:1	Key Verse: 3:1	Key Verse: 4:1	Key Verses: 5:1-3	Key Verse: 6:11
1	2	3	4	5:1–6:10	6:11-21

As Timothy was pastoring the church in Ephesus, Titus was overseeing the church on the island of Crete, and Philemon was evidently leading a church meeting in his home. The letters to these three men indicate that Paul was deeply concerned that they live lives of godliness and lead their churches with wisdom. From your reading today, respond to the following statements and questions.

How would you describe the tone of the apostle Paul in this letter?

For the ignorant, old age is as winter; for the learned, it is a harvest.

—Jewish proverb

List one or two statements or verses that caught your attention.

What do you hope to learn from your study of 1 Timothy this week?

MEMORY VERSE

I write so that you will know how one ought to conduct himself in the household of God, which is the church of the living God.

1 TIMOTHY 3:15

REVIEW IT
The theme of 1 Timothy is leadership of a local church.

I Timothy
[Instructions on Leadership]

THINK ABOUT IT
The greatest Leader
who ever lived said,
"[I] did not come to be
served, but to serve"
(Mark 10:45).

DAY TWO

COMPLETE READ: Chapters 1–2
QUICK READ: Passages in this day's lesson

NOTABLE FEATURE NUMBER 1

> These are hard times in which a genius would wish to
> live. Great necessities call forth great leaders.
> —ABIGAIL ADAMS, WIFE OF JOHN ADAMS,
> WRITING TO THOMAS JEFFERSON IN 1790

The apostle Paul knew well the "hard times" in which young
Timothy was ministering. He also knew that "great necessities
call forth great leaders" and that "as the leader goes, so go the
people." So in this letter, the experienced church planter exhorts
an inexperienced church pastor to greatness.

But Paul's exhortation is not only to a way of leading but also to
a way of living. It is not only to a code of conduct but also to a
concentration on character. It is not only to a litany of leadership
principles but also to a life of spiritual development. Paul knew
that a spiritual leader must pay attention to both what he does
and who he is. Our Notable Feature Number 1 is that character
and conduct cannot be separated.

Three passages in particular zero in on these issues for
Timothy. Read each of them and respond to the questions and
statements provided for you.

4:7-16

List the many exhortations Paul gives Timothy and briefly

*You must be careful
how you walk, and
where you go, for there
are those following you
who will set their feet
where yours are set.*

—ROBERT E. LEE, U.S.
Confederate general in
the Civil War

explain what you think Paul's main point or concern was for each one.

If you could make one summary statement about all of these, what would it be?

5:1-3

Paul refers to five classes of people. What are they, and why do you think he encourages Timothy to respond to each one as he does?

6:11-16

Use as many words and phrases as you can to describe Paul's tone in this section.

Look not at the shape, look at the character.
—Turkish proverb

How does this section differ from the previous two?

Explain how the phrase "character is everything" fits with this passage.

Being a good example
Doing everything in love.

Many times exhortations to leaders are just as applicable to followers. Whether you view yourself as a leader or a follower, what major truth has the Holy Spirit impressed on your heart through this study?

REVIEW IT!
Notable Feature Number 1 is that character and conduct cannot be separated.

MEMORY VERSE

I write so that you will know how one ought to conduct himself in the household of God, which is the church of the living God.

1 TIMOTHY 3:15

I TIMOTHY
[Instructions on Leadership]

DAY THREE

COMPLETE READ: Chapters 3–4
QUICK READ: Chapter 5

NOTABLE FEATURE NUMBER 2

In his commentary on Paul's letters to Timothy, Titus, and Philemon, William Barclay quotes Philo, a philosopher of Alexandria, writing about our responsibility to honor our parents: "When old storks become unable to fly, they remain in their nests and are fed by their children, who go to endless exertions to provide their food."[1] Barclay also quotes Aristotle: "It would be thought in the matter of food we should help our parents before all others, since we owe our nourishment to them, and it is more honorable to help in this respect the authors of our being, even before ourselves."[2]

The early church had inherited the Greek cultural tradition of caring for aged parents. The Jews also contributed a centuries-long history of similar concern and care. These were strong positive models to follow for the early Christians. Yet apparently one specific group of aging parents needed to be addressed by Paul for the benefit of the church at large: widows. In the original Greek, the words *widow* and *widows* occur nine times in all of Paul's letters, and eight of those occurrences are in 1 Timothy 5. This is our Notable Feature Number 2: caring for widows in the church.

It is true, as the passage teaches, that family members are the first line of care and support for widows, but many times and for many reasons, the church must be involved. Very early in the history of the church, a problem developed concerning the care

THINK ABOUT IT
In the New Testament era, a woman of sixty was generally considered aged and infirm!

Let all find compassion in you.
—SAINT JOHN OF THE CROSS, sixteenth-century Carmelite monk

of widows (see Acts 6). Evidently it was a large enough challenge that Paul felt compelled to spell out detailed instructions for their care.

In 1 Timothy 5:3-16, Paul describes five types of widows. They are listed below along with the verses in which they are discussed. Read the verses and write down everything you learn about each type of widow, including how each was to be treated.

A widow indeed (verses 3,5,16)

INTERESTING!
When a polygamist became a Christian, he had to choose which wife to live with, creating, in a sense, widows.

A widow who has a family (verses 4,8,16)

A widow who lives in wanton pleasure (verses 6-7)

A widow who is on the list (verses 9-10)

Note: Evidently there was an official registry of widows in the early church that functioned as a way for the widows to receive care and to be unified as a group for special ministry duties.

This only is charity, to do all, all that we can.

—JOHN DONNE,
clergyman and poet

A younger widow (verses 11-15)

Write down any thoughts you have about this teaching on the care of widows and the parallels, or lack thereof, that you see in the church today.

Has a particular widow come to your mind during your study today? If so, write down her name. Has this passage encouraged you to do something in relation to this person? If so, what?

If you are a widow, write down a particular time when someone cared for you in a way that brought you comfort. Thank God for that.

Memory Verse

I write so that you will know how one ought to conduct himself in the household of God, which is the church of the living God.

1 Timothy 3:15

REVIEW IT!
Notable Feature Number 2 is the importance of caring for widows in the church.

I TIMOTHY
[Instructions on Leadership]

DAY FOUR

COMPLETE READ: Chapter 5
QUICK READ: Passages in this day's lesson

NOTABLE FEATURE NUMBER 3

Thumb through the pages of the Old Testament, and the names, lives, and importance of women leap out with great regularity and significance:

- Eve, the mother of mankind

- Sarah, the wife of possibly the most important man in the Old Testament and the mother of the child of promise, Isaac

- Rahab, a key link in the conquest of Jericho and a member of the genealogy of Jesus

- Ruth, the model of loyalty and trust; also in the line of Jesus

- Esther, the single-handed savior of thousands of Jews at a critical juncture in their history

Turn to the New Testament and find more significant women:

- Mary, the mother of Jesus

- Mary Magdalene, the first person to see the risen Christ

- The four women who stood by Christ at all costs as He hung on the cross

- Priscilla, who with her husband played a significant role in early church teaching

- The four daughters of Philip who were prophetesses

UNBELIEVABLE!
In the morning prayer, a Jewish man thanked God that he had not been made a Gentile, a slave, or a woman.

Being a woman is a terribly difficult trade, since it consists principally of dealing with men.

—JOSEPH CONRAD, Polish-born English novelist and short-story writer

All throughout Scripture women held places of honor and made significant impacts. And the list we've just reviewed is merely representative.

Even so, among both the Jews and the Greeks, the official status of a woman was very low. In Jewish life, a woman was at the disposal of her father or husband, was allowed no part in the religion of the synagogue, was classed with children and slaves, and was never greeted by a rabbi in public. In the Greek world, women were used in religion as sacred prostitutes or were confined to their own quarters, never being allowed to appear in public alone.

So the high scriptural view and the low cultural view of women stand in stark contrast. And into this setting come the teachings of Paul in 1 Timothy. Other than his first letter to the church at Corinth, no other Pauline epistle addresses issues about women as extensively as the one we are now studying. In the original language, the words *woman* or *women* appear ten times in these six chapters, and that does not include the extended passage about widows that we studied yesterday. Paul's emphasis on women is our Notable Feature Number 3.

Paul's teaching about women in this letter is controversial even today. It is outside the scope of this study to investigate all the contemporary issues involved. But as you reflect upon the following passages, prayerfully rely on the Holy Spirit, who inspired these words, to give you insight into them. Read the passages and then respond to the questions and statements.

2:9-12

Note: In regard to verse 9, there were some women in Greek society who spent all of their time focused on dressing elaborately and braiding their hair ostentatiously.

What does Paul instruct women to do?

HIGH HONOR
Four women are listed in Jesus' genealogy in Matthew 1.

No one knows like a woman how to say things which are at once gentle and deep.
—Victor Hugo, French dramatist, novelist, and poet

What does Paul instruct women *not* to do?

What does this mean to you?

3:11 (notice the context of verses 1-12)

In your own words, describe the woman of verse 11.

5:2 (notice the context of verse 1)

What does this verse say about Paul's view of women?

What has been most challenging for you in this study? How can you verbalize it in prayer to God?

MEMORY VERSE

I write so that you will know how one ought to conduct himself in the household of God, which is the church of the living God.

1 TIMOTHY 3:15

I TIMOTHY
[Instructions on Leadership]

DAY FIVE

COMPLETE READ: Chapter 6
QUICK READ: Chapter 6

REMEMBER
Money is amoral. It
is equally suited to
produce either good
or evil.

A TIMELESS PRINCIPLE

In his excellent book *Money, Possessions and Eternity*, Randy Alcorn records the testimonies of five very wealthy men:

- John D. Rockefeller: "I have made many millions, but they have brought me no happiness."

- W. H. Vanderbilt: "The care of $200,000,000 is enough to kill anyone. There is no pleasure in it."

- John Jacob Astor: "I am the most miserable man on earth."

- Henry Ford: "I was happier when doing a mechanic's job."

- Andrew Carnegie: "Millionaires seldom smile."[3]

If a man's religion does not affect his use of money, that man's religion is vain.
—HUGH MARTIN

Money and contentment. How often in our finite, human minds we link the two. Our value structures compel us to pursue money with the expectation that it will produce contentment, or we pursue contentment by obsessing over money. Yet both these paths lead to a dead end. In 1 Timothy 6, Paul addresses these issues as a necessary part of any leadership manual for a local church. Paul's famous statement about money is often misquoted, and that misquote has become a cliché in our culture: "Money is the root of all evil." His actual statement is, "The love of money is a root of all sorts of evil" (verse 10). Handling money in a godly manner is a Timeless Principle.

First Timothy 6 includes two sections that deal with this topic. The first passage gives a warning and focuses primarily on the negative. The second passage provides instruction and places an emphasis on the positive.

Read the passages given and then respond to the questions and statements that follow each one.

6:6-10

Summarize these verses by listing the principles you see about money and contentment.

What "evil" have you seen or experienced as a result of "the love of money"?

6:17-19

Using your own words, state what these verses say.

He will always be a slave who does not know how to live upon a little.

—HORACE, Roman lyric poet and satirist

What contrasts do you see between these two passages?

Even Solomon, one of the richest men to ever live, discovered the truth about money and contentment. In Ecclesiastes 5:10-11, he wrote,

> He who loves money shall never have enough. The foolishness of thinking that wealth brings happiness! The more you have, the more you spend, right up to the limits of your income. So what is the advantage of wealth — except perhaps to watch it as it runs through your fingers! (TLB)

What continued reflection and possible action might God be impressing on you as a result of this study?

MEMORY VERSE

I write so that you will know how one ought to conduct himself in the household of God, which is the church of the living God.

1 TIMOTHY 3:15

O eternal God, though Thou art not such as I can see with my eyes or touch with my hands, yet grant me this day a clear conviction of Thy reality and power. Let me keep steadily in mind that the things that matter are not money or possessions, not houses or lands, not bodily comfort or bodily pleasure; but truth and honor and meekness and helpfulness and a pure love of Thyself.

—JOHN BAILLIE, Scottish theologian and ecumenical leader

I TIMOTHY
[Instructions on Leadership]

REVIEW

1. The theme of 1 Timothy is ___*leadership*___ of a local church.

2. Notable Feature Number 1 is that character and ___(Behavior) Conduct___ cannot be separated.

3. Notable Feature Number 2 is the importance of caring for ___Widows___ in the church.

4. Notable Feature Number 3 is Paul's emphasis on ___Women___.

5. "I write so that you will know how one ought to ___Conduct___ himself in the household of God, which is the church of the living God."

1 TIMOTHY 3:___15___

2 TIMOTHY

[*Instructions on Endurance*]

You therefore, my son, be strong in the grace

that is in Christ Jesus.

2 TIMOTHY 2:1

2 Timothy
[Instructions on Endurance]

INTRODUCTION

Paul's second letter to Timothy reads very differently from his first. First Timothy is about the church the young pastor was leading; 2 Timothy is about the young pastor who was leading the church. First Timothy is about the structure, order, and programs of the church; 2 Timothy is about the character, endurance, and faithfulness of the pastor, Timothy.

It is easy to identify with Timothy. He was carrying so much on his shoulders, and in this letter we get the sense that he was beginning to sag a bit. Not only was the load heavy, but some of the responsibilities he was charged with were either outside his comfort zone or needed to be carried out in the face of opposition.

Paul could not physically come to his rescue; he was old, he was in prison, and he was about to be martyred. So he did what he could do, something he did so well — he wrote Timothy a letter of encouragement, challenge, warning, reminder, and love. No one knew Timothy better than Paul, and no one could address his needs more incisively and concisely.

The beauty of the apostle's writing under the inspiration of the Holy Spirit is that, even though his letter was a personal one to Timothy, when we read it, it feels as if it were written especially for us. May you benefit from the impact of this letter in your life this week.

2 TIMOTHY
[Instructions on Endurance]

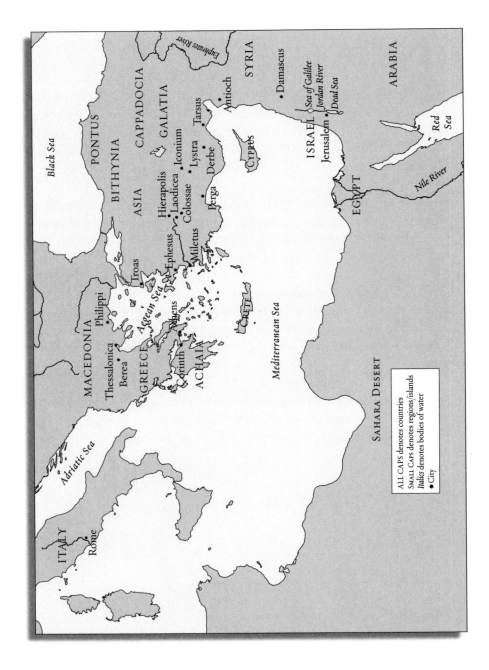

2 TIMOTHY
[Instructions on Endurance]

OVERVIEW

WHO: Author: Paul
Main Character: Timothy

WHAT: Timothy's commissioning letter and combat manual for endurance

WHEN: AD 67

WHERE: Written from prison in Rome to Timothy in Ephesus

WHY: To prepare Timothy for the growing opposition he would face in his ministry and to encourage him to endure hardships and possible persecution

I. PAUL GAVE TIMOTHY THE CHARACTERISTICS OF "THE MAN OF GOD" (2 TIMOTHY 1–2).

    A. Paul greeted Timothy as his beloved _____ in the faith.

    B. Paul _____ Timothy with loving words.

    C. Timothy was reminded of his _____ and of God's enabling power.

    D. The qualifications of a _____ of Christ were described.

    E. Timothy was told how to be a _____ pleasing to Christ.

II. PAUL GAVE TIMOTHY CAUTIONS FOR "THE MAN OF GOD" (2 TIMOTHY 3).

    A. Know the _____ of the last days.

    B. _____ suffering as Paul had done because:

        1. The Lord was faithful to _____ him.

        2. All who desire to live for Christ will be _____ .

        3. _____ men will go from bad to worse — deceiving and being deceived.

C. Timothy must _____ in what he had learned and remember from whom and where he learned it.

D. All Scripture is "God breathed," or _____ .

E. Scripture is valuable because:

    1. It teaches by explaining what's _____ .

    2. It reproves by explaining what's _____ .

    3. It corrects by explaining how to _____ .

    4. It instructs by explaining how to _____ .

    5. It completes and _____ "the Man of God" for kingdom work.

III. PAUL CHALLENGED TIMOTHY WITH A CHARGE FOR "THE MAN OF GOD" (2 TIMOTHY 4).

A. Timothy was charged to:

    1. _____ the good news.

    2. Be _____ at all times to instruct people.

    3. _____ those who are doing wrong.

    4. _____ sinners with stern reprimands.

    5. _____ with great patience and careful teaching.

B. A time would come when people would no longer listen to _____ but would desire teachers who would say what they wanted to hear.

C. Paul's last letter to Timothy ends with very _____ words.

APPLICATION

There is growing opposition to Christianity today. Stand firm on the principles of God's Word to endure hardships and possible persecution.

2 TIMOTHY
[Instructions on Endurance]

LEARNING FOR LIFE

1. What is the theme of the book, and why is this so?

2. How are we encouraged in this letter with words about suffering and persecution? As a student of God's Word, how should we prepare our children by teaching this truth?

3. How important is it to you that you sit under true teaching and that you in turn rightly handle the Word of God (see 2 Timothy 2:15)?

4. In 2 Timothy 3, Paul lists signs of "the last days." Which of these are you seeing today? What does this say about the truth of God's Word?

5. How does Paul's example of living as "a man of God" inspire and challenge you?

2 TIMOTHY
[Instructions on Endurance]

DAY ONE

COMPLETE READ: Chapters 1–4

QUICK READ: Chapters 1–4

THE BIG PICTURE

*Encouragement is the
oxygen of the soul.*
—GEORGE M. ADAMS,
American author of the
twentieth century

Paul was in prison; Timothy was in Ephesus. From Paul to
Timothy, from prison to Ephesus came a letter of encouragement, emotion, exhortation, example, and endurance.

Paul's relationship with Timothy had been long and intimate.
So when Paul wrote to his young friend (undoubtedly within
months of his martyrdom), the apostle's heart was exposed.
He assured Timothy of his love and ceaseless prayer for him.
Knowing Timothy's timidity, he nudged him on to boldness,
perseverance, and faithfulness to his calling, whatever the cost.

Paul reminded Timothy of some ill-advised behaviors in his
position: Do not pursue youthful lusts, do not haggle over words,
do not be unkind. But above all, the great apostle was concerned
for truth and the faithful and constant preaching of the Word of
God. Timothy had been taught well, and Paul reminded him to
remember this teaching. Paul exhorted him to handle the Word
of truth accurately and diligently. Timothy would come across
those who would want to hear only what they wanted to hear,
and Paul commanded him not to give in to that pressure.

Like a soldier, Timothy was to please the one who enlisted him.
As an athlete, Timothy was to compete according to the rules.
And as a farmer, Timothy ought to be the first to receive his
share of the crops.

This description of the message of 2 Timothy uncovers the

theme of the book: endurance of a man of God. It is possible to view the call to endurance through three lenses:

CHARACTERISTICS of the Man of God	CAUTION for the Man of God	CHARGE to the Man of God
"You therefore, my son, be strong in the grace that is in Christ Jesus." (2:1)	"You, however, continue in the things you have learned." (3:14)	"I solemnly charge you in the presence of God and of Christ Jesus." (4:1)
1–2	3	4

Five years had passed since Paul's release from his first imprisonment in Rome. During those years, Paul traveled to places such as Ephesus, Rome, Macedonia, Spain, Crete, Greece, and Asia Minor. He also wrote his first letter to Timothy and one to Titus. But as he wrote 2 Timothy, he was once again imprisoned in Rome. The year was around AD 67.

Three years earlier, Nero had burned Rome and pinned the blame on the Christians. As a result, being a Christian and associating with the leaders of Christianity became a dangerous business. Many believers purposely sought lower profiles as a means of self-protection. In the midst of this environment, Paul sent this letter encouraging his young son in the faith, Timothy, to endure. This was Paul's last letter, written just months before his death as a martyr at the hands of Rome.

Who would wish for hardship and difficulty? You command us to endure these troubles, not to love them. No one loves what he endures even though he may be glad to endure it.
—SAINT AUGUSTINE OF HIPPO, Carthaginian author and church father

Paul's tone is serious—and urgent. He no doubt realized this imprisonment would have a very different result from the one five years previous. At that time he was accused by the Jews as a heretic; this time he was treated by the Romans as a criminal. Then he was held under house arrest in somewhat comfortable quarters; now he was incarcerated in a cold, damp, underground prison cell. At that time he shared the gospel freely with those who visited him; this time his friends could see him only with much difficulty and danger. Then he anticipated release from prison; now he expected release only through his death.

Nothing great was ever done without much enduring.

—CATHERINE OF SIENA, fourteenth-century Italian mystic

Some have called this letter Paul's last will and testament. In this sense, these four chapters are similar to the gospel of John, chapters 13–17. Those words were spoken by Jesus to His chosen apostles on the evening of His arrest leading to His crucifixion and death. They were His last words to the men He loved so much and to whom He was entrusting the future of His ministry. Likewise, Paul was writing to Timothy, whom he dearly loved and to whom he also was entrusting the continuation of his ministry.

With this in mind, place yourself in Timothy's sandals. As he reread this letter after the great apostle's death, what words and phrases do you think would have stood out as especially significant, considering they were Paul's last words to him? Quickly scan these chapters and write down those words and phrases.

Ask God in prayer to give you an urgent endurance in life and ministry as you study this letter.

MEMORY VERSE

You therefore, my son, be strong in the grace that is in Christ Jesus.

2 TIMOTHY 2:1

REVIEW IT!
The theme of 2 Timothy is the endurance of a man of God.

2 TIMOTHY
[Instructions on Endurance]

DAY TWO

COMPLETE READ: Chapter 1
QUICK READ: Passages in this day's lesson

UNDERSTANDABLE
Second Timothy is the
most personal of Paul's
four pastoral letters.

A KEY INSIGHT

Scan the Christian living section of your local religious bookstore, and you will be amazed and overwhelmed by the different avenues of advice available to encourage you in your walk with God. Some authors will stress the study and understanding of the truth of God's Word. Others will focus on becoming the kind of person God wants you to become. Still others will advocate a more active approach, claiming that doing, serving, and being involved in ministry is the key that unlocks the door to spiritual maturity.

In reality, all three components are necessary for spiritual maturity. They can be summarized as follows:

KNOW	BE	DO
Study and Learn Truth	Pursue Growth in Character	Be Involved in Ministry
HEAD	HEART	HANDS

As we acquire more knowledge, things do not become more comprehensible, but more mysterious.

—ALBERT SCHWEITZER, French missionary, philosopher, and physician

These three emphases by no means exhaust the challenging and at times mysterious privilege of walking with God, but they do offer a way to think about our spiritual life and growth. Thus, our Key Insight is that knowing, being, and doing are all important in our walk with God.

THINK ABOUT IT
Our temperament type
tends to steer us more
naturally to either
know, be, or do.

Interestingly, all three are strongly emphasized by Paul in this letter to his young friend Timothy. He directly commands Timothy to know, be, and do. Scan the book for Paul's commands and write them down with their references under the appropriate heading. Keep in mind that some can be placed in more than one category depending on how you see them. This is fine. The process is more important than the product. An example is given for each one.

KNOW

Example: "Consider what I say, for the Lord will give you understanding in everything" (2:7).

BE

Example: "Now flee from youthful lusts" (2:22).

One must not always think so much about what one should do, but rather what one should be. Our works do not ennoble us; but we must ennoble our works.

—MEISTER ECKHART, second-century Christian mystic

DO

Example: "Do the work of an evangelist" (4:5).

As you review this study, what area do you gravitate to most naturally?

Least naturally?

Is the Holy Spirit impressing upon you the need to adjust any aspect of your spiritual walk? If so, what is He leading you to change? How will you respond?

Deliberation is the work of many people. Action, of one alone.

—CHARLES DE GAULLE, French general and politician

MEMORY VERSE

You therefore, my son, be strong in the grace that is in Christ Jesus.

2 TIMOTHY 2:1

REVIEW IT!
Our Key Insight is that knowing, being, and doing are all important in our walk with God.

2 TIMOTHY
[Instructions on Endurance]

DAY THREE

COMPLETE READ: Chapter 2
QUICK READ: Chapter 2

A PROMINENT PLAYER

Paul had many friends and coworkers, but none of them surpassed Timothy in his intimacy with and importance to Paul. The love the apostle had for this young man was that of a father to a son. Indeed, Paul was Timothy's father — his spiritual father. Timothy is our Prominent Player for today's study.

Timothy was a native of Lystra in the province of Galatia. Even though it was just a little town at the end of civilization, it called itself the most brilliant colony of Lystra. William Barclay, in his commentary on the Pastoral Epistles, writes, "Its importance was that there was a Roman garrison quartered there to keep control of the wild tribes of the Isaurian mountains which lay beyond."[1] Paul and Barnabas visited Lystra on the first missionary journey, but no mention was made of Timothy. But when Paul returned to Lystra on his second missionary journey, life changed for this young servant of God.

How green you are and fresh in this old world.
—WILLIAM SHAKESPEARE, *King John*

Again Barclay writes, "On that first visit Timothy must have been very young, but the Christian faith laid hold upon him, and Paul became his hero. . . . Young as he was, he had become one of the ornaments of the Christian church in Lystra. . . . To Paul he seemed the very man to be his assistant."[2]

Paul's second visit is recorded in Acts 16:1-3. Read these verses and write down what you learn about Timothy.

What does 2 Timothy 1:5 add to your understanding of Timothy's background?

DID YOU KNOW?
In Roman culture, a person was considered young until age forty.

From the time of this Acts 16 encounter, Paul and Timothy remained very close companions. Timothy's name appears in the salutations of Paul's letters more than any other person's. Here are some examples of Timothy's importance to Paul:

- Paul left him behind to minister at Berea when Paul escaped to Athens.

- He later joined Paul in Athens.

- Paul sent him as his personal representative to Macedonia.

- He was present when the collection from the churches was taken to Jerusalem.

- He was with Paul in Corinth when the apostle penned Romans.

- He was Paul's representative to Corinth when that church was overcome by internal problems.

- Paul sent him to check out the situation in the Thessalonian church.

- He was with Paul in prison.

A number of passages clearly show how Paul felt about Timothy. Read the following passages and record what you learn about Timothy and also Paul's thoughts and feelings about him.

1 Corinthians 4:17

When we think of friends, and call their faces out of the shadows, and their voices out of the echoes that faint along the corridors of memory, and do it without knowing why save that we love to do it, we content ourselves that friendship is a Reality, and not a Fancy — that it is built upon a rock, and not upon the sands that dissolve away with the ebbing tides and carry their monuments with them.

—DOUGLAS FAIRBANKS, American movie actor and first president of the Academy of Motion Picture Arts and Sciences

1 Corinthians 16:10-11

Philippians 2:19-24

What do the following passages indicate about Timothy?

1 Timothy 4:12; 2 Timothy 2:22

1 Timothy 5:23

2 Timothy 1:6-8; 2:1-3

In a role that required maturity, Timothy was young. In a situation that called for physical stamina, Timothy was somewhat sickly. And in a position that demanded boldness, Timothy was timid. What does that say to you about the kind of people God can use for His great purposes?

Is there a specific encouragement you need to take from this truth?

MEMORY VERSE

You therefore, my son, be strong in the grace that is in Christ Jesus.

2 TIMOTHY 2:1

2 TIMOTHY
[Instructions on Endurance]

DAY FOUR

COMPLETE READ: Chapter 3
QUICK READ: Chapter 3

A NOTABLE FEATURE

In his classic book *Life Together*, Dietrich Bonhoeffer writes, "Let him who cannot be alone beware of community. He will only do harm to himself and to the community. . . . But the reverse is also true: Let him who is not in community beware of being alone. . . . In the community of the called you bear your cross, you struggle, you pray."[3]

The last fourteen verses of 2 Timothy (4:9-22) are a personal presentation of these truths. In these verses, Paul mentions no less than seventeen individuals by name and adds, "all the brethren." Community was undoubtedly important, even crucial, to Paul. But within the language of community, the passage also indicates that when he wrote this letter to Timothy, Paul sensed that he was very much alone. Paul would surely shout hearty agreement with Bonhoeffer's words. Both community and solitude are used by God in our lives to fashion us into the kind of people He wants us to be. Our Notable Feature of 2 Timothy is Paul's experience of community and solitude at the end of his life.

The disturbing truth of these verses, and probably of your life as well, is that at times, the people who are part of your community can also be the hurtful cause of your feelings of solitude. For example, Alexander receives the most attention in this last chapter of 2 Timothy. The phrase Paul used to describe him in verse 14, "did me much harm," means literally "to display." Many

AMAZING!
Paul remained a student even when he knew death was just around the corner (2 Timothy 4:13).

The person who tries to live alone will not succeed as a human being. His heart withers if it does not answer another heart. His mind shrinks away if he hears only the echoes of his own thoughts and finds no other inspiration.

—PEARL S. BUCK,
American novelist and Pulitzer prize–winning author

times this phrase is used in regard to information brought by one man against another. Informants abounded in Rome during this time, and it is possible that Alexander was one who turned against Paul during the time of Nero's persecution of Christians. Read 4:14-15 and respond to the following statements.

In your own words, record Paul's response to Alexander in verses 14-15.

CHECK IT OUT
Check out the "lovers of" phrase in 2 Timothy 3:2-4. How many times did you find it written?

Verses 16-18 most likely refer to others who also deserted Paul. It is spiritually instructive to study Paul's response to these desertions. Describe in your own words Paul's attitude and hope in this time of solitude.

Another relational disappointment for Paul was Demas. Read Philemon 23-24 and Colossians 4:14 and write down what Paul's relationship to Demas seems to have been.

Within the wider fellowship emerges the special circle of a few on whom, for each of us, a particular emphasis of nearness has fallen.

—THOMAS KELLY, twentieth-century Quaker missionary, scholar, and speaker

Now read 2 Timothy 4:10, written about five years after the previous two references, and describe in your own words the situation with Demas.

In the midst of Paul's depressing and discouraging solitude, there was a surprising delight of community. Mark is mentioned in 4:11. Paul's relationship with Mark had a long history. Read the following verses and summarize each.

Acts 12:25 (AD 47–48)

Acts 13:13 (Summer AD 48)

Acts 15:36-41 (Spring AD 50)

Colossians 4:10 (Autumn AD 61)

We have no information about the relationship between Paul and Mark from AD 50 to 61, but somehow it had been repaired. As a result, in 2 Timothy 4:11 (AD 67), Paul specifically desired Mark to be with him at the end of his life.

Community can be confusing, and there never seems to be a shortage of hurt as we journey together. Yet Paul's personal testimony is that God will uphold and at times even heal broken relationships. You likely have at least one story from your life that mirrors this passage. Describe it to the best of your ability and then lay yourself before God for His strengthening.

MEMORY VERSE

You therefore, my son, be strong in the grace that is in Christ Jesus.

2 TIMOTHY 2:1

REVIEW IT!
Our Notable Feature in 2 Timothy is Paul's experience of community and solitude.

2 TIMOTHY
[Instructions on Endurance]

The word *inspired* in
2 Timothy 3:16 literally
means "God-breathed."

DAY FIVE

COMPLETE READ: Chapter 4
QUICK READ: Chapter 4

A TIMELESS PRINCIPLE

Psalm 119, the longest chapter in the Bible, elevates and affirms
the critical importance of God's Word in all but one of its 176
verses. A few of those verses describe the timeless nature of the
Word:

> Forever, O LORD,
> Your word is settled in heaven. (verse 89)

> Of old I have known from Your testimonies
> That You have founded them forever. (verse 152)

> The sum of Your Word is truth,
> And every one of Your righteous ordinances is
> everlasting. (verse 160)

*Defend the Bible? I
would as soon defend a
lion! Unchain it and it
will defend itself.*
—CHARLES SPURGEON,
nineteenth-century
British preacher

Not only is God's Word timeless; our need for the truth of
that Word is also timeless—a Timeless Principle. Listen to the
psalmist again:

> Your Word is a lamp to my feet
> And a light to my path. (verse 105)

> The unfolding of Your words gives light;
> It gives understanding to the simple. (verse 130)

Establish my footsteps in Your word,
And do not let any iniquity have dominion over
me. (verse 133)

Second Timothy 3:16-17 is a classic passage on the Word of God, the Bible. In these few words, Paul communicates three truths regarding the Word of God: its source, its profit, and its results. For each of the italicized words and phrases below, write out your understanding of its meaning.

ITS SOURCE

Inspired by God

REMEMBER
Only two things from earth will last for eternity: people and the Word of God.

ITS PROFIT

Teaching

Reproof

Correction

Training in righteousness

We cannot rely on the doctrine of Scripture until we are absolutely convinced that God is its author.

—JOHN CALVIN, sixteenth-century French Protestant reformer and theologian

Its Results

Adequate

Equipped for every good work

Describe your current personal relationship to the Bible, that is, your reading of it, studying it, meditating on it, or memorizing of it.

Describe the role you believe the Bible has played in your spiritual life.

What one step could you take to increase the impact of the Scriptures in your life? How will you incorporate this step into your habits and schedule?

The authority of Scripture must be followed in all things, for in it we have the truth as it were in its secret haunts.

—JOHN SCOTUS ERIGENA, Scottish philosopher and theologian

MEMORY VERSE

You therefore, my son, be strong in the grace that is in Christ Jesus.

2 TIMOTHY 2:1

2 TIMOTHY
[Instructions on Endurance]

REVIEW

1. The theme of 2 Timothy is the _____ of a man of God.

2. Our Key Insight is that knowing, _____ , and doing are all important in our walk with God.

3. Our Prominent Player is _____ .

4. Our Notable Feature in 2 Timothy is Paul's experience of _____ and solitude.

5. "You therefore, my son, be strong in the _____ that is in Christ Jesus."

2 TIMOTHY 2:_____

TITUS

[Instructions on Church Order]

Speak confidently, so that those who have believed God

will be careful to engage in good deeds.

TITUS 3:8

THREE

TITUS
[Instructions on Church Order]

INTRODUCTION

In this third letter to pastoral leaders in the early church, Paul wrote to Titus. Titus assumed leadership responsibility for the infant church on Crete, an island in the Mediterranean Sea southeast of Greece. Titus's major challenge was the culture in which he was ministering. Over the years, the people there had developed a corporate personality and character that made finding church leaders of integrity very difficult. According to Titus 1:12, "One of themselves, a prophet of their own, said, 'Cretans are always liars, evil beasts, lazy gluttons.'"

As a result, Paul reiterated to Titus what he had written to Timothy about the indispensable character traits and ministry abilities required of men who were to serve as elders. Following these instructions, Paul instructed Titus what to expect of and how to mentor various groups of people in the church: older men, older women, young men, and bondslaves. His description of the goal for older women in 2:3-5 has been used by numerous women's ministries as a guideline for the relationships between older and younger women in the church. You will study this passage as our Timeless Principle on Day Five.

Another part of Paul's instruction to Titus, in 2:11-14, regards the all-encompassing grace of God. You will reflect on this passage on Day Four as a Notable Feature of this epistle.

This short letter has so much to offer: encouragement, instruction, and challenge. Expect to be blessed as you study!

TITUS
[Instructions on Church Order]

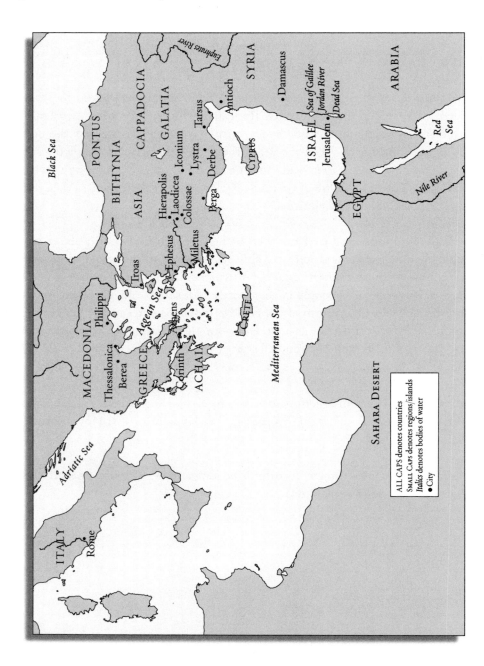

TITUS
[Instructions on Church Order]

OVERVIEW

Who: Author: Paul
Main Character: Titus

What: A letter of instruction to the church and its leaders

When: AD 63

Where: Written from Paul, perhaps in Corinth, to Titus on the Mediterranean island of Crete

Why: To provide encouragement, exhortation, and instruction on maintaining sound doctrine as leaders and as a body of believers

I. THE PROTECTION OF SOUND DOCTRINE IN THE CHURCH (TITUS 1)

A. Paul instructed Titus to ordain qualified _____ in the church.

    1. _____ — bishops; had special responsibilities to superintend; pastors

    2. _____ — senators; older ones; appointed by apostles; had spiritual giftedness

    3. _____ — servants of someone; helpers; practical agents

B. Paul ordered Titus to choose leaders whose overall _____ was blameless.

    1. _____ — with their wives and children at home

    2. _____ — respected in the community and at work

    3. _____ — know and show the Word

C. Paul encouraged Titus to rebuke the _____ teachers in the church.

II. THE PRACTICE OF SOUND DOCTRINE IN THE CHURCH (TITUS 2)

   A. Paul directed Titus to teach the older men and women to _____ the younger men and women.

      1. _____ — to advise; to instruct; suggests a close relationship between elder and younger

      2. _____ — to give hope; to urge on; to help develop; to exhort

      3. _____ — to give a visible impression; to illustrate; to show quality or characteristics

      4. _____ — to give verbal instruction; to impart knowledge or information

      5. _____ — to reprove sharply; to correct; to bring to light; to expose wrong

   B. Paul insisted that Titus train the younger men and women to be
      _____ .

   C. Paul told Titus to teach slaves to be _____ and trustworthy.

III. THE PARTICIPATION IN SOUND DOCTRINE IN THE WORLD (TITUS 3)

   A. Paul required all members to _____ the law of the land.

   B. Paul reminded the believers why they should do profitable, _____ works.

   C. Paul demanded that the congregation avoid _____ and useless works.

APPLICATION

An orderly, Christ-committed church will not only know but proclaim the Word to the world.

TITUS
[Instructions on Church Order]

LEARNING FOR LIFE

1. Sum up the main thrust of Paul's famous last words to Titus and the church in Crete. What are the famous last words you would like to pass on to others?

2. Do you agree with Paul's list for leaders? Why or why not? What character traits do you look for in a leader?

3. Why was it so important for the church to have mentors training and teaching others to know and show the Word?

   a. Do you think this would be valuable in your life?

   b. Are you willing to mentor or be mentored?

4. What are some practical ways you can show an unbelieving world what you know about God?

TITUS
[Instructions on Church Order]

PERSPECTIVE
Crete was 156 miles long and 30 miles wide at its broadest point.

DAY ONE

COMPLETE READ: Chapters 1–3
QUICK READ: Chapters 1–3

THE BIG PICTURE

Just as Timothy was pastor in the church at Ephesus, Titus was pastor in the church on the island of Crete. Titus is not mentioned in the book of Acts but is mentioned thirteen times in Paul's epistles. Briefly review the following references and write down what you learn about him in each one.

2 Corinthians 2:12-13

2 Corinthians 7:6-7

Order is heaven's first law.

—ALEXANDER POPE,
English poet and satirist

2 Corinthians 8:16-17

2 Corinthians 8:23

2 Corinthians 12:18

Galatians 2:1

2 Timothy 4:10

REVEALING
"To Cretize" was
synonymous with
"to lie."

Titus 1:4

Summarize what you have learned about Titus.

Cretans were present in Jerusalem at the time of Pentecost and heard Peter's stirring sermon (see Acts 2:11). Possibly a number of them believed the gospel at that time and introduced it to their island when they returned home. Despite this, the people of Crete had a reputation for lying, unrighteousness, and rebellion.

*Take but degree away,
untune that string
And hark what discord
follows.*
—WILLIAM SHAKESPEARE,
Troilus and Cressida

Evidently Paul was not able to minister there until after his release from his first Roman imprisonment in AD 62. We do not know how long he stayed, but it appears the church was already functioning with Titus as its leader when Paul arrived (Titus 1:5). Within a year (AD 63), Paul wrote this letter to Titus to instruct and strengthen him in his challenging job of bringing order to a church located on an island that was well-known for general disorderliness (1:12).

Paul advised him to appoint elders to help him in this endeavor. But they had to be chosen carefully. They needed to be men who were above reproach in their personal lives, faithful in their families, sound in their doctrine, and able to rebuke and exhort in their teaching.

But the elders were not the only group of individuals in the church with a clear mandate. Older men were to live lives of dignity, faith, and love; older women were to forsake gossip and teach the younger women what it meant to be godly wives and mothers; young men were to pursue traits of wisdom and maturity; and slaves were to respond in ways that pleased their masters.

So even though the responsibility for leadership was placed on the shoulders of qualified godly elders, everyone in the body was to approach his or her walk with God with seriousness and commitment in the midst of a hostile environment.

Our theme for Titus is order in the church. The following chart shows one way to look at the contents of this letter.

Order in the Church Leadership	Order in the Church Congregation
Responsibilities and Character of the Elders	Responsibilities and Character of Older Men, Older Women, Young Men, Bondslaves, All Members
1	2–3

From your brief exposure to this book, write down two or three ideas, statements, or words that seem a bit different from the other books we have studied thus far. Is there something here you should pursue on your own if we do not address it in this study?

MEMORY VERSE

Speak confidently, so that those who have believed God will be careful to engage in good deeds.

TITUS 3:8

TITUS
[Instructions on Church Order]

DAY TWO

COMPLETE READ: Chapters 1–3
QUICK READ: Passages in this day's lesson

INSIGHT
The expression "to play the Cretan with a Cretan" meant "to outtrick a trickster."

A CRUCIAL PASSAGE

You have heard the expression that in real estate, the three most important factors are location, location, and location. And in leadership, the three most important factors are character, character, and character. In their book *The Ascent of a Leader*, coauthors Bill Thrall, Bruce McNicol, and Ken McElrath state, "Character — the inner world of motives and values that shapes our action . . . empowers our capacities while keeping them in check. It distinguishes those who steward power well from those who abuse power. Character weaves such values as integrity, honesty, and selfless service into the fabric of our lives."[1]

I love the name of honor more than I fear death.
—WILLIAM SHAKESPEARE, *Julius Caesar*

From what we know about the Cretans, character was not a top cultural priority. In fact, they seemed to revel in its lack. Therefore, our Crucial Passage, Titus 1:5-9, is very apropos in Paul's letter to his young friend. It describes the qualifications required of a man if he was to serve as an elder or overseer in the church. This is not the first time Paul gave this instruction for the appointment of elders. About a year earlier, he wrote similar words in his first letter to his other young friend, Timothy. We postponed investigating that passage until we got to the book of Titus so we could study the two together.

The topic of leadership in the church today is such a crucial issue that we will take two days to reflect on these passages in 1 Timothy 3:1-7 and Titus 1:5-9. Depending on their particular denomination, tradition, or theology, churches give different titles to individuals holding leadership positions. Regardless of the title, the three most important qualifications are character, character, and character. This is the major (but not the only) thrust of these passages.

Combining the two passages presents us with twenty-one traits by which to evaluate, choose, and train church leaders. We will list each trait and the verses where it is found and give a short definition of its biblical meaning. For each, write down some of your own thoughts of what it means and how it would be manifested. Then write down the name of one or two church leaders you believe model this trait well.

Above reproach (1 Timothy 3:2; Titus 1:6-7): having a good reputation

Husband of one wife (1 Timothy 3:2; Titus 1:6): exhibiting moral purity

Character is what you are in the dark.
—DWIGHT L. MOODY,
American evangelist

Temperate (1 Timothy 3:2): having a clear focus on life, stable, steadfast, not indulging the appetites

Prudent/sensible (1 Timothy 3:2; Titus 1:8): sound in mind, discrete, sober

Respectable (1 Timothy 3:2): orderly, well-arranged

Hospitable (1 Timothy 3:2; Titus 1:8): sharing one's home and other possessions

Able to teach (1 Timothy 3:2; Titus 1:9): demonstrating the ability to communicate with others in a nonargumentative, nondefensive, and nonthreatening way (as opposed to merely being able to stand up and teach a group)

We will conclude this study tomorrow. Hopefully you are remembering and beginning to appreciate a number of individuals God has placed in leadership over you.

MEMORY VERSE

Speak confidently, so that those who have believed God will be careful to engage in good deeds.

TITUS 3:8

REVIEW IT!
Our Crucial Passage is Titus 1:5-9, which speaks about the traits of mature church leaders.

TITUS
[Instructions on Church Order]

POSSIBILITY
Zenas and Apollos probably delivered this letter to Titus (Titus 3:13).

DAY THREE

COMPLETE READ: Chapters 1–3
QUICK READ: Passages in this day's lesson

A CRUCIAL PASSAGE (CONTINUED)

Yesterday we began our study of the traits of individuals who are placed in positions of leadership in the church (for example: elder, overseer, bishop). As you have studied these characteristics and given thought to those you know who embody them, you may have begun to realize that it is very profitable to think about yourself in relationship to these traits, whether you are in a position of leadership or not.

Continue your study of these traits by using the same process you began yesterday.

Not addicted to wine (1 Timothy 3:3; Titus 1:7): not prone to drink too much or to be in bondage

It takes a long time to bring excellence to maturity.

—PUBLILIUS SYRUS, first-century BC Latin writer of mime plays

Not self-willed (Titus 1:7): not self-centered, self-pleasing, or arrogant

Not quick-tempered (Titus 1:7): not prone to loss of temper or prolonged anger

Not pugnacious (1 Timothy 3:3; Titus 1:7): does not let his anger get out of control, does not strike

DID YOU KNOW?
Titus is commemorated in the Western church on January 4, in the Eastern church on August 25.

Gentle (1 Timothy 3:3): forbearing, fair, kind, meek

Peaceable (1 Timothy 3:3): not argumentative or quarrelsome

Free from the love of money/not fond of sordid gain (1 Timothy 3:3; Titus 1:7): generous, not greedy, nonmaterialistic

Manages his own household well/has children who believe (1 Timothy 3:4-5; Titus 1:6): has a home committed to Jesus Christ with grown children who respect and love their father

Good reputation with those outside the church (1 Timothy 3:7): above reproach in the eyes of unbelievers

I'm not afraid of storms, for I'm learning to sail my ship.
—LOUISA MAY ALCOTT, American novelist

Loving what is good (Titus 1:8): desiring to do what is good, not what is evil

Just (Titus 1:8): wise, discerning, able to make mature and proper judgments in relationships with others

Devout (Titus 1:8): exhibits holiness lived out in behavior

Self-controlled (Titus 1:8): has self-mastery

Not a new convert (1 Timothy 3:6): has been a believer long enough for maturity to develop

Remember, the gospel says, "Well done, good and faithful servant" (Matthew 25:21, NIV), not "perfectly done, faultless and infallible servant." These traits are to be present and growing, but we aren't talking about perfection. We are still talking about people — imperfect people.

Take time to write a note of affirmation to those individuals you have thought about as you did this study. Also write down one thing that challenged you personally. Is there a response you should make?

REVIEW IT!
Again, our Crucial Passage is Titus 1:5-9, which speaks about the traits of mature church leaders.

MEMORY VERSE

Speak confidently, so that those who have believed God will be careful to engage in good deeds.

TITUS 3:8

TITUS
[Instructions on Church Order]

DAY FOUR

COMPLETE READ: Chapters 1–3
QUICK READ: Chapters 1–3

A NOTABLE FEATURE

Philip Yancey relates the story of religious experts from around the world who convened in Great Britain to try to determine if there was any one belief that was unique to Christianity. They ran the gamut of suggestions with no success until, as Yancey records, "C. S. Lewis wandered into the room. 'What's the rumpus about?' he asked, and heard in reply that his colleagues were discussing Christianity's unique contribution among world religions. Lewis responded, 'Oh, that's easy. It's grace.'"[2] All the scholars had to agree.

Only Christianity flies the flag of grace for everyone far and wide to see. And in this very short letter to Titus, Paul uses nine of the forty-six verses to speak of grace. In reality, it is the needed counterbalance to the other verses. Because of the nature of the other material — commands, instructions, exhortations, warnings — these two short passages stand out as lifesaving reminders that whatever we are asked to be or do will come to fruition *only* by the grace of God. What's different about Christians? "Oh, that's easy. It's grace."

The two passages in Titus are 2:11-14 and 3:4-8. Read and reflect on 2:11-14 and respond to the following questions and statements.

These verses talk about grace in three tenses: past, present, and future. Write down the words that apply to each tense and record your own commentary on their meaning.

SIGNIFICANT
Of the book of Titus,
Martin Luther said
that it contained "all
that is necessary for a
Christian to know and
live by."

Past

Present

Future

Look at verse 12 again. In your own experience, how does the grace of God enable you "to deny ungodliness and worldly desires and to live sensibly, righteously and godly in the present age"?

If I am not [in a state of grace], God bring me there; if I am, God keep me there!

—JOAN OF ARC, French heroine, military leader, and saint

Now read the second passage, 3:4-8, and respond to the following questions and statements.

Verses 4-7 appear to be an expansion of 2:11. Discuss the ways in which they fill out our understanding of the grace of God bringing salvation to all men in 2:11.

What does 3:7 add to the future aspect described in 2:13?

Interestingly, 3:5 says, "Not on the basis of deeds which we have done," while 3:8 says, "Be careful to engage in good deeds." In your own words, explain how both of these statements are true.

Take time to write a short prayer to God expressing your feelings about His grace that *has* saved you, that *is* helping you to live in a godly way, and that *will be* displayed fully when Christ returns.

Memory Verse

Speak confidently, so that those who have believed God will be careful to engage in good deeds.

TITUS 3:8

TITUS
[Instructions on Church Order]

REMEMBER
The "self-made"
woman is a myth.

DAY FIVE

COMPLETE READ: Chapters 1–3
QUICK READ: Chapter 2

A TIMELESS PRINCIPLE

With all the technological and nonrelational approaches to learning and training available to us over the last several decades, person-to-person mentoring had begun to fade in popularity and status. Thankfully, mentoring is experiencing a sort of rebirth in our culture today. Business leaders are encouraging it as a means of raising up the next generation of leaders. Spiritual writers are advocating it as the way to pass the baton of spiritual vitality to the next church in the making. Socially conscious individuals are promoting it as the method to take something beneficial ingrained in one life and transfer and build it into another life.

Mentoring is a good and powerful thing. And it has been around for a long time. Moses mentored Joshua. Socrates mentored Plato. Paul mentored Timothy. The idea and practice of mentoring is our Timeless Principle.

Our chief want is someone who will inspire us to be what we know we could be.
—RALPH WALDO EMERSON, nineteenth-century American essayist and poet

Interestingly, tucked away in the second chapter of Titus is a strong passage on mentoring: older women mentoring younger women. No ages are attached to "older" and "younger," so almost everyone is eligible to fill the role of either the older or the younger woman. Most of us can find others ahead of us and behind us in life.

This passage is found in Titus 2:3-5. Verse 3 describes the traits desirable in older women, and verses 4-5 describe what the older women should encourage the young women to be and do. We will study the verses in this order. The various characteristics and reasons for their importance are printed with space for you to describe in your own words what they mean. You may have questions about some of them. You may feel ambivalent, anxious, or defensive about one or two of them. This is good. It gives you the opportunity to struggle with issues that Paul, under the inspiration of the Holy Spirit, felt were important enough to include.

OLDER WOMEN

Reverent in their behavior

Not malicious gossips

Not enslaved to much wine

Teaching what is good

Reason: That they may encourage the young women

YOUNG WOMEN

Love their husbands

Love their children

Tell me what company you keep, and I'll tell you what you are.
—MIGUEL DE CERVANTES, sixteenth-century Spanish writer, playwright, and poet

Sensible

Pure

Workers at home

Kind

Subject to their own husbands

Reason: That the Word of God will not be dishonored

Are you a young woman seeking an older woman to mentor you? Are you an older woman who seeks to build godly qualities in a young woman? Whatever your situation, pray that you will be sensitive and receptive to God's leading in your heart.

Don't wait for someone to take you under their wing. Find a good wing and climb up underneath it.

—FRANK C. BUCARO, author and speaker on business and leadership ethics

MEMORY VERSE

Speak confidently, so that those who have believed God will be careful to engage in good deeds.

TITUS 3:8

TITUS
[Instructions on Church Order]

REVIEW

1. The theme of Titus is _____ in the church.

2. Our Crucial Passage is Titus 1:5-9, which speaks about the traits of mature church
   _____ .

3. Again, our Crucial Passage is Titus 1:5-9, which speaks about the _____
   of mature church leaders.

4. Our Notable Feature of Titus is Paul's strong emphasis on _____ .

5. "Speak confidently, so that those who have _____ God will be
   careful to engage in good deeds."

   TITUS 3:_____

PHILEMON

[Instructions on Forgiveness]

If then you regard me a partner,

accept him as you would me.

PHILEMON 17

FOUR

PHILEMON
[Instructions on Forgiveness]

INTRODUCTION

While Paul's letters to Timothy and Titus cover many different ideas, his short epistle to Philemon zeroes in on one issue. If we were to say the previous letters were written from a shotgun approach, this one is the work of a rifle. One shot, one target.

The letter is written from one leader, Paul, to another leader, Philemon, and it speaks of an issue every leader must model for his or her followers: forgiveness. Forgiving others may be one of life's most difficult challenges, but at the same time it is one of the most necessary. The issue Philemon was involved in is one in which, culturally speaking, a person would not have been expected to extend forgiveness. The story involves a slave owner being asked to forgive and take back his runaway slave.

Paul raised the bar on forgiveness in his request to Philemon. And believing, as he did, in the integrity and character of his friend, he expected nothing but a positive response.

In Philemon, we see a huge truth coming from a small book. Blessings on you this week as you reflect on this truth, which is rooted in the very heart of God Himself and is one He modeled so perfectly for us.

PHILEMON

[Instructions on Forgiveness]

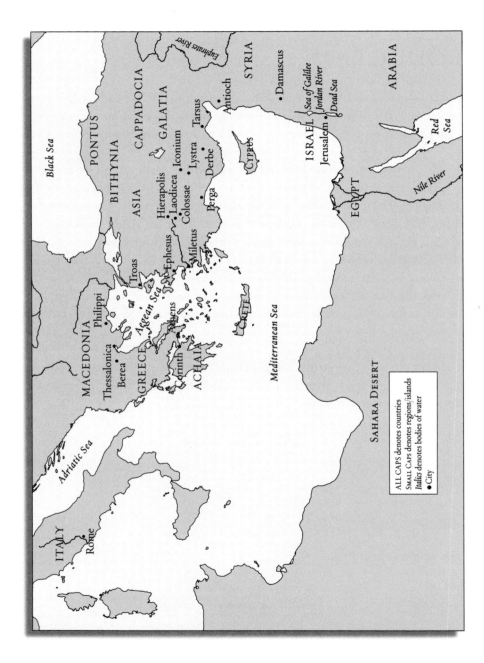

PHILEMON
[Instructions on Forgiveness]

OVERVIEW

WHO: Author: Paul
Main Characters: Philemon, Onesimus

WHAT: A letter to Philemon regarding the forgiveness of his runaway slave, Onesimus

WHEN: AD 61

WHERE: Written from prison in Rome to Philemon in Colossae

WHY: To live out Christian love and forgiveness

SEVEN REASONS TO BELIEVE THE BIBLE:

1. _____ : The sixty-six books were written by forty authors over 1,500 years, but they tell one unified story.

2. _____ : The Bible claims to be God's Word written by men moved by the Spirit.

3. _____ : Tests of archaeology and bibliography have never refuted it.

4. _____ : Prophecy of the Bible has been fulfilled.

5. _____ : Man's many attempts to destroy it have failed (see Mark 13:31).

6. _____ : The Bible's influence on society has been more positive than any other book.

7. _____ : Individual lives have been transformed by it.

I. PHILEMON'S CHARACTER PRAISED (PHILEMON 1-7)

A. Philemon was Paul's beloved_____ and fellow worker.

B. Philemon's_____ met in his house.

C. Philemon had great faith toward God and_____ toward the saints.

II. Philemon's Character Tested (Philemon 8-20)

A. Paul appealed to Philemon on behalf of Philemon's_____, Onesimus.

B. Onesimus became_____ . He stole from Philemon and ran away.

C. In Christ, Onesimus became_____ . He ministered to Paul.

D. Paul appealed to Philemon to_____ Onesimus as a brother in the Lord.

E. Paul offered to_____ Onesimus's debt.

III. Philemon's Character Trusted (Philemon 21-25)

A. Paul was confident Philemon would be_____ and do more than asked.

B. Paul was confident Philemon's_____ would free him from prison.

IV. Lessons We Learn from Philemon

A. We need to be_____ .

B. It is not enough to be forgiven; we must also_____ .

C. Once forgiven, we must make_____ .

Application

Who do you need to forgive? What do you need to make right?

PHILEMON
[Instructions on Forgiveness]

LEARNING FOR LIFE

1. What is the theme of the book of Philemon?

2. As a group, briefly recap the story.

3. Who in this story is like you? How are you the same?

4. Who in this story is like Jesus? How are they the same?

5. What did you learn today about forgiveness?

6. Briefly share about a time when you forgave someone or made restitution.

PHILEMON
[Instructions on Forgiveness]

TO THE POINT
Philemon is the shortest of Paul's letters.

DAY ONE

COMPLETE READ: Verses 1-25
QUICK READ: Verses 1-25

THE BIG PICTURE

Philemon's impact far exceeds its size. In just twenty-five verses, we have a complete portrayal of forgiveness not unlike the forgiveness we receive from Jesus Christ.

The characters in this story are as follows:

- Philemon: a slave owner

- Onesimus: a runaway slave owned by Philemon

- Paul: a friend of Philemon and the person God used to bring spiritual conversion to Onesimus

Onesimus had not only run away from Philemon, but he had also taken property that belonged to his master (verse 18). Once Onesimus became a believer under Paul's preaching, he served Paul in prison. Paul was now sending him back to his master with this letter, asking Philemon to take his slave back, forgive him, and, if necessary, send Paul a bill for anything Onesimus might owe that he was unable to pay.

Our theme of Philemon is forgiveness and restoration. The likeness of our eternal forgiveness by God is all here: sin, compassion, intercession, substitution, restoration, and a new relationship. The chart that follows provides one possible outline of this short but very personal letter.

Life is an adventure in forgiveness.

—NORMAN COUSINS, writer, editor, diplomat, and author

Paul's APPRECIATION of Philemon Key Verse: 7	Paul's APPEAL to Philemon Key Verse: 10	Paul's CONFIDENCE in Philemon Key Verse: 21
Philemon's Character Praised	Philemon's Character Tested	Philemon's Character Trusted
1 7	8 20	21 25

NOTICE
In contrast to his other epistles, Paul wrote Philemon entirely in his own hand (Philemon 19).

This unique letter of Paul to Philemon was written in AD 61 during Paul's first Roman imprisonment (Philemon 9-10,13), the same time Ephesians, Colossians, and Philippians were written. Many scholars believe that Apphia (verse 2) was Philemon's wife and that Archippus (verse 2) was Philemon's son.

There is a significant connection between the books of Philemon and Colossians. Read Philemon 1-2 and Colossians 4:7-9,17. Then trace the statements below back to these passages to see if you agree with them.

- Philemon lived in the city of Colossae.

- Archippus was apparently responsible for some specific ministry in the church.

- Philemon hosted a church in his home.

- Tychicus hand-delivered two letters from Paul in prison to the city of Colossae.

- The slave, Onesimus, traveled with Tychicus.

- Paul expected Philemon to respond positively to his request regarding Onesimus.

Some estimates state there were as many as sixty million slaves in the Roman Empire. In those days, a slave was at the absolute mercy of his master. For the smallest offense a slave could be scourged, mutilated, crucified, or thrown to wild beasts.[1] Apparently, many Christians owned slaves and many slaves became Christians because Paul addressed both groups throughout his letters, giving regulations regarding the treatment of

The weak can never forgive. Forgiveness is the attribute of the strong.
—MAHATMA GANDHI, Indian nationalist leader and political activist

slaves by their owners and the conduct of slaves to their masters (see Ephesians 6:5-9; Colossians 3:22–4:1).

As you have studied this introduction to the book of Philemon, has God been prompting your heart about any issues related to forgiveness in your life? Are there people you have never forgiven? Partially forgiven? Refused to forgive? Simply neglected to forgive? Are there those who have not forgiven you? Write down their names and any thoughts about forgiveness you have at this time.

MEMORY VERSE

If then you regard me a partner, accept him as you would me.

PHILEMON 17

 PHILEMON
[Instructions on Forgiveness]

DAY TWO

COMPLETE READ: Verses 1-25
QUICK READ: Passages in this day's lesson

WOW!
In this short book of only twenty-five verses, Paul mentions eleven people besides himself.

NOTABLE FEATURE NUMBER 1

You've heard it many times: People don't care how much you know until they know how much you care. The giving or receiving of care — concern, attention, interest, tenderness — is one of the most powerful lubricants for smooth-functioning relationships.

If there is any place in Paul's thirteen epistles where he not only teaches but also models this self-giving, caring attitude, it is in this short, heartfelt letter to his friend Philemon. D. Edmond Hiebert, in his book *An Introduction to the Pauline Epistles*, writes that in this display of "Paul's devoted love to individual souls we may discover one of the secrets of his success as a missionary. It was because of his affectional personal interest in men wherever he went that the apostle was able to exercise such a powerful grip upon the hearts of his friends."[2] What Hiebert calls Paul's "affectional personal interest" is another way of saying that his friends knew how much he cared. Our Notable Feature Number 1 is Paul's caring heart.

Spend some time reflecting on and *feeling* the contents of this brief letter. Then respond to the following questions and statements.

True affection is ingeniously inventive.

—FRANÇOIS FÉNELON,
seventeenth-century
French bishop
and author

Write down as many words and phrases as you can that describe Paul's "affectional personal interest" toward Philemon.

Write down as many words and phrases as you can that describe Paul's "afffectional personal interest" toward Onesimus.

Our Lord does not care so much for the importance of our works as for the love with which they are done.

—Saint Teresa of Avila, Spanish mystic and Carmelite nun

This may be a bit more difficult to see (and you may need to think through the implications), but write down as many sentiments as you can that show Paul's "affectional personal interest" for the broader cause of Christians and Christianity in the world.

We are familiar with the terms IQ (intelligence quotient) and EQ (emotional quotient), but maybe we should also think of our CQ (caring quotient). If someone you know well were to write a paragraph describing your CQ, what kinds of things might that person include in his or her comments?

MEMORY VERSE

If then you regard me a partner, accept him as you would me.

PHILEMON 17

REVIEW IT!
Our Notable Feature
Number 1 is Paul's
caring heart.

PHILEMON
[Instructions on Forgiveness]

DAY THREE

COMPLETE READ: Verses 1-25
QUICK READ: Passages in this day's lesson

NOTABLE FEATURE NUMBER 2

Do you believe great things come in small packages? Think diamonds! They are small, yet stunning, meaningful, valuable, and cherished. The same is true about this small package called The Letter of Paul to Philemon. The truth wrapped up in this small literary parcel is stunning, meaningful, valuable, and to be cherished.

Think diamonds again. They not only are all the things we've already mentioned, but they also display different facets of their dazzling beauty depending on how we turn them in the light. The same is true of this diamond of truth called Philemon. Turn it different ways, allowing the light of reality to strike it, and different facets of its dazzling beauty will be displayed.

Our Notable Feature Number 2 is the large value of this small letter.

W. Graham Scroggie creatively and meaningfully summarizes the many facets of this book's value. The rest of this study will be based on Scroggie's words; the italics have been added for emphasis. After each segment of his quote, reflect on the content and message of Philemon and write down appropriate thoughts, questions, or opinions.

I know the Bible is inspired because it finds me at a greater depth of my being than any other book.
—SAMUEL TAYLOR COLERIDGE, English poet

"Its *personal* value consists in the light which it throws upon the character of Paul."

"Its *ethical* value consists in its balanced sensitiveness to what is right."

"Its *providential* value consists in its underlying suggestion that God is behind and above all events."

"Its *practical* value consists in its application of the highest principles to the most common affairs."

"Its *evangelical* value consists in the encouragement it supplies to seek and to save the lowest."

COUNT 'EM
In the original Greek, the word *brother* occurs four times in this short book, two times with the adjective *beloved*.

We must allow the Word of God to confront us, to disturb our security, to undermine our complacency and to overthrow our patterns of thought and behavior.
—JOHN STOTT, author and Christian leader

"Its *social* value consists in its presentation of the relation of Christianity to slavery and all unchristian institutions."[3]

Now complete this sentence: Its personal value to *me* consists in . . .

REVIEW IT!
Our Notable Feature Number 2 is the large value of this small letter.

MEMORY VERSE

If then you regard me a partner, accept him as you would me.

PHILEMON 17

PHILEMON
[Instructions on Forgiveness]

DAY FOUR

COMPLETE READ: Verses 1-25
QUICK READ: Passages in this day's lesson

A TIMELESS PRINCIPLE

Because our Timeless Principle is so important, we will spend two days studying and reflecting upon it.

In *The Sunflower*, Simon Wiesenthal recalls days from his time in the German death camps. One day a wounded German, near death, asked to be able to speak to a Jew. Wiesenthal was the Jew they brought to his side. The German recounted how he had mercilessly killed numbers of men, women, and children and had been unable to shake memories of the horror he had caused and witnessed. He longed for forgiveness from another Jew who would in some way substitute for those who obviously could not grant him that gift.

Wiesenthal listened to the man's pleas but refused to forgive him. Yet his refusal haunted him, so he contacted thirty-two professional scholars and psychologists. Of each one he asked, "Should I have forgiven the man on his deathbed for the crime he had confessed to committing?" Twenty-six of the thirty-two told Wiesenthal he had done the right thing by refusing to forgive the German.[4]

Can you identify with the choice to hold back the gift of forgiveness, especially when the deed to be forgiven is so horrendous?

INTERESTING!
Philemon is all about forgiveness, even though the word never occurs in the letter.

The man who is truly forgiven and knows it, is a man who forgives.
—M. LLOYD-JONES, author and preacher

It is at times like these that we are tempted to defer to the words of the eighteenth-century English poet Alexander Pope, who wrote,

> Good-nature and good-sense must ever join;
> To err is human, to forgive, divine.[5]

To be sure, to err *is* human, but to forgive is also human — at least in God's view:

> Do not grieve the Holy Spirit of God. . . . Be kind to one another, tender-hearted, forgiving each other, just as God in Christ also has forgiven you. (Ephesians 4:30,32)

> So, as those who have been chosen of God, holy and beloved, put on a heart of compassion, kindness, humility, gentleness and patience; bearing with one another, and forgiving each other, whoever has a complaint against anyone; just as the Lord forgave you, so also should you. (Colossians 3:12-13)

The common denominator in these two passages is the similar phrasing at the end of each: "just as God in Christ also has forgiven you" and "just as the Lord forgave you." This is our Timeless Principle: We forgive as God has forgiven us. This is what Paul was asking Philemon to do.

It is through Christ's death in our place to pay for our sins that God has forgiven us. Amazingly, during His horrific death, Jesus modeled forgiveness *twice*. Read Luke 23:32-43 and respond to the following questions and statements.

How would you describe what Jesus was going through? You may want to consult the other gospels for more details of Jesus' painful ordeal.

*I as free forgive you as
I would be forgiven.
I forgive all.*

WILLIAM SHAKESPEARE,
Henry VIII

Describe Jesus' two acts of forgiveness in this passage.

What does this say to you about forgiveness? Remember, we are to forgive others "just as God in Christ" has forgiven us — thoroughly and completely.

What is most difficult for you in forgiving others? Does this passage speak to your difficulty? If so, how?

MEMORY VERSE

If then you regard me a partner, accept him as you would me.

PHILEMON 17

REVIEW IT!
Our Timeless Principle is that we forgive as God has forgiven us.

PHILEMON
[Instructions on Forgiveness]

VOCABULARY
The verb *forgive* literally means "to send away."

DAY FIVE

COMPLETE READ: Verses 1-25
QUICK READ: Passages in this day's lesson

A TIMELESS PRINCIPLE (CONTINUED)

Fulton Ousler Jr. was nineteen when his father died. During the last years of his father's life, Fulton Jr. had worked closely with his dad doing typing and research. His father had become a Christian late in life and was writing articles about his newfound life in Christ. Fulton Jr. was also responsible for his father's library, thousands of volumes and over two hundred personal notebooks.

After his father's death, he discovered a small spiral notebook he had never seen before with page after page of nothing but carefully printed names. There were names of family members, friends, and even some people who had already died. Following a blank page he found a list of about twenty names, most of which he did not recognize. When he showed the spiral notebook to his mother, she said it was his father's prayer book and that every night before he turned out the light, he opened the book, put his finger on each name, and prayed silently. When young Ousler asked who the twenty people on the last list were, she said, "They were people who had hurt him."

Again, our Timeless Principle is that we forgive as God has forgiven us.

The remainder of this study will involve reflection on your part — and writing down whatever is appropriate.

Here in the presence of Almighty God, I kneel in silence, and with penitent and obedient heart confess my sins, so that I may obtain forgiveness by Your infinite goodness and mercy. Amen.

—The Book of Common Prayer

Read Matthew 5:9-13. What do you think verse 12 means?

POSSIBILITY
One tradition supposes
that Onesimus the
runaway slave became
Onesimus the bishop
of Ephesus!

Read Matthew 18:21-22. What thoughts do you have as you read these words of Jesus Christ?

Describe two or three instances in which you have consciously and clearly forgiven another person.

Describe two or three instances in which you were clearly forgiven by another person.

We are certain that there is forgiveness, because there is a gospel, and the very essence of the gospel lies in the proclamation of the pardon of sin.
—CHARLES SPURGEON, nineteenth-century British preacher

Are you withholding forgiveness from any people who have hurt you? If so, are you willing to write their names down and put into words why you will not forgive them?

Is there anything you have not forgiven yourself for?

As a result of this reflection, is there someone or something you need to honestly deal with before God and by His grace?

I think that if God forgives us we must forgive ourselves.

—C. S. Lewis, British essayist, novelist, and Christian apologist

Memory Verse

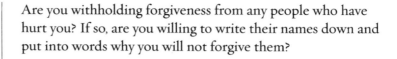

If then you regard me a partner, accept him as you would me.

PHILEMON 17

PHILEMON
[Instructions on Forgiveness]

REVIEW

1. The theme of Philemon is _____ and restoration.

2. Our Notable Feature Number 1 is Paul's _____ heart.

3. Our Notable Feature Number 2 is the large value of this small _____ .

4. Our Timeless Principle is that we _____ as God has forgiven us.

5. "If then you regard me a _____ , accept him as you would me."

PHILEMON _____

Comprehensive Review of
Paul's Letters to Pastors

1 Timothy

1. The theme of 1 Timothy is _____ of a local church.

2. Notable Feature Number 1 is that character and _____ cannot be separated.

3. Notable Feature Number 2 is the importance of caring for _____ in the church.

4. Notable Feature Number 3 is Paul's emphasis on _____ .

5. "I write so that you will know how one ought to _____ himself in the household of God, which is the church of the living God."

1 Timothy 3:_____

2 Timothy

1. The theme of 2 Timothy is the _____ of a man of God.

2. Our Key Insight is that knowing, _____ , and doing are all important in our walk with God.

3. Our Prominent Player is _____ .

4. Our Notable Feature in 2 Timothy is Paul's experience of _____ and solitude.

5. "You therefore, my son, be strong in the _____ that is in Christ Jesus."

2 TIMOTHY 2:_____

TITUS

1. The theme of Titus is _____ in the church.

2. Our Crucial Passage is Titus 1:5-9, which speaks about the traits of mature church _____ .

3. Again, our Crucial Passage is Titus 1:5-9, which speaks about the _____ of mature church leaders.

4. Our Notable Feature of Titus is Paul's strong emphasis on _____ .

5. "Speak confidently, so that those who have _____ God will be careful to engage in good deeds."

TITUS 3:_____

PHILEMON

1. The theme of Philemon is _____ and restoration.

2. Our Notable Feature Number 1 is Paul's _____ heart.

3. Our Notable Feature Number 2 is the large value of this small _____ .

4. Our Timeless Principle is that we _____ as God has forgiven us.

5. "If then you regard me a _____ , accept him as you would me."

PHILEMON _____

CONGRATULATIONS!

You have just completed set ten, Paul's Letters to Pastors, and fifty-seven books of the Bible. You've studied all the recorded letters that the apostle Paul wrote to the churches and to pastors. His life was a testimony to the awesome power of Jesus Christ working through one man totally yielded to Him. Paul was a man who lived and died for Christ, who truly poured himself out as an offering to his Savior. His life as revealed in his letters serves as an incredible example and inspiration to all believers.

There are many hints in Paul's letters that persecution against Christians was growing. Many of the letters written in set eleven, Other Letters and Revelation, were written at a somewhat later date and strongly urged Christians to stand firm even in the midst of growing opposition. Another problem addressed frequently in these letters is that of false teaching. Even in the early years of the church, false teachers were working to delude believers into accepting doctrines that were not true.

The final nine books were written by several different authors, including John and Peter, the disciples of Jesus Christ. These books contain added teachings on the Christian life, such as how to deal with suffering and trials, what fellowship with Christ looks like, and why Christ is superior to the angels, Moses, the prophets, and the law.

The last book is the book of Revelation, which offers believers a panoramic view of what will take place when Jesus Christ returns to judge the earth and claim His bride, the church. Revelation's picture ends with a new heaven and a new earth where Christ reigns with His bride. It is a book of majesty and terror, of devastation and great promise.

So the adventure continues. Only one more set of books to go, and we will have reached our goal! We continue to pray that this study has helped you learn what every book in the Bible is about and that you have come to love more dearly the God of the Bible and His Son, Jesus Christ. The end is in sight. Now press on!

CHRONOLOGICAL RELATIONSHIP OF THE NEW TESTAMENT BOOKS

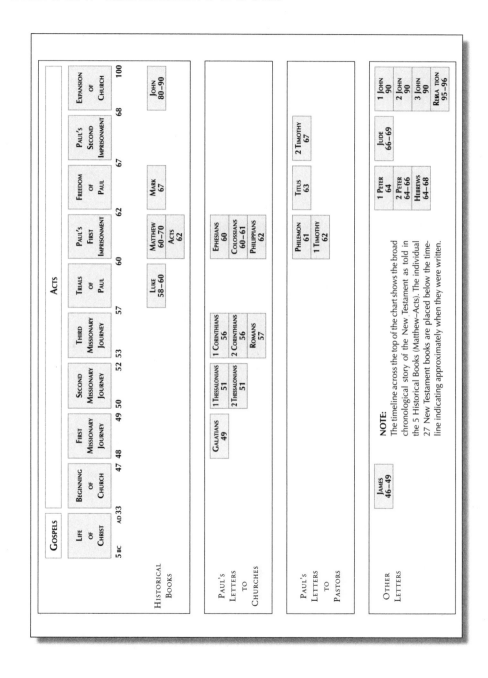

HISTORICAL BOOKS

GOSPELS

			ACTS									
LIFE OF CHRIST	BEGINNING OF CHURCH	FIRST MISSIONARY JOURNEY	SECOND MISSIONARY JOURNEY	THIRD MISSIONARY JOURNEY	TRIALS OF PAUL	PAUL'S FIRST IMPRISONMENT	FREEDOM OF PAUL	PAUL'S SECOND IMPRISONMENT	EXPANSION OF CHURCH
5 BC AD 33	47 48	49 50	52 53	57	60	62	67	68	100

LUKE 58–60

MATTHEW 60–70
ACTS 62

MARK 67

JOHN 80–90

PAUL'S LETTERS TO CHURCHES

GALATIANS 49

1 THESSALONIANS 51
2 THESSALONIANS 51

1 CORINTHIANS 56
2 CORINTHIANS 56
ROMANS 57

EPHESIANS 60
COLOSSIANS 60–61
PHILIPPIANS 62

PAUL'S LETTERS TO PASTORS

PHILEMON 61
1 TIMOTHY 62

TITUS 63

2 TIMOTHY 67

OTHER LETTERS

JAMES 46–49

1 PETER 64
2 PETER 64–66
HEBREWS 64–68

JUDE 66–69

1 JOHN 90
2 JOHN 90
3 JOHN 90
REVELATION 95–96

NOTE:
The timeline across the top of the chart shows the broad chronological story of the New Testament as told in the 5 Historical Books (Matthew–Acts). The individual 27 New Testament books are placed below the timeline indicating approximately when they were written.

THE FIRST MISSIONARY JOURNEY OF PAUL

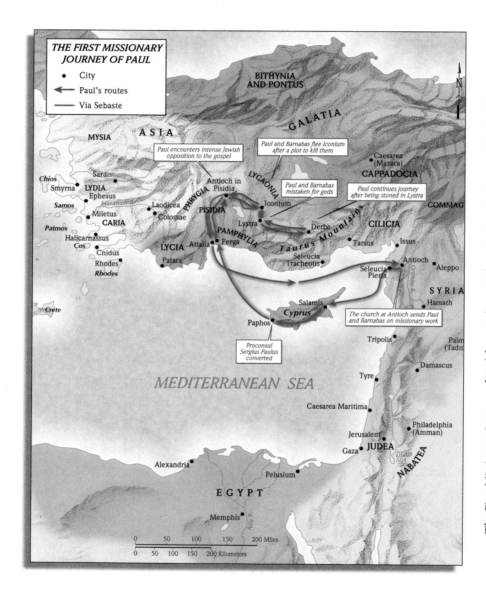

THE FIRST MISSIONARY JOURNEY OF PAUL

- • City
- ← Paul's routes
- — Via Sebaste

BITHYNIA AND PONTUS

GALATIA

MYSIA

ASIA

Chios
Smyrna
LYDIA
Sardis
Ephesus
Maeander
Samos
Miletus
Laodicea
CARIA
Colossae
Patmos
Halicarnassus
Cos
Cnidus
Rhodes
Rhodes

PHRYGIA
PISIDIA
Antioch in Pisidia

LYCAONIA

Caesarea (Mazaca)
CAPPADOCIA

COMMAG

Paul encounters intense Jewish opposition to the gospel

Paul and Barnabas flee Iconium after a plot to kill them

Paul and Barnabas mistaken for gods

Iconium

Paul continues journey after being stoned in Lystra

Lystra

Derbe

CILICIA

Tarsus

Issus

PAMPHYLIA
LYCIA
Attalia
Perga
Patara

Taurus Mountains

Seleucia Tracheotis

Antioch
Aleppo

Seleucia Pieria
Orontes R.

SYRIA
Hamath

Salamis

Cyprus

The church at Antioch sends Paul and Barnabas on missionary work

Paphos

Proconsul Sergius Paulus converted

Tripolis

Palm (Tadm

Damascus

Tyre

MEDITERRANEAN SEA

Caesarea Maritima

Crete

Philadelphia (Amman)

Jerusalem
Gaza
JUDEA
DEAD SEA
NABATEA

Alexandria

Pelusium

EGYPT

Memphis
Nile R.

0   50   100   150   200 Miles
0   50   100   150   200 Kilometers

THE SECOND MISSIONARY JOURNEY OF PAUL

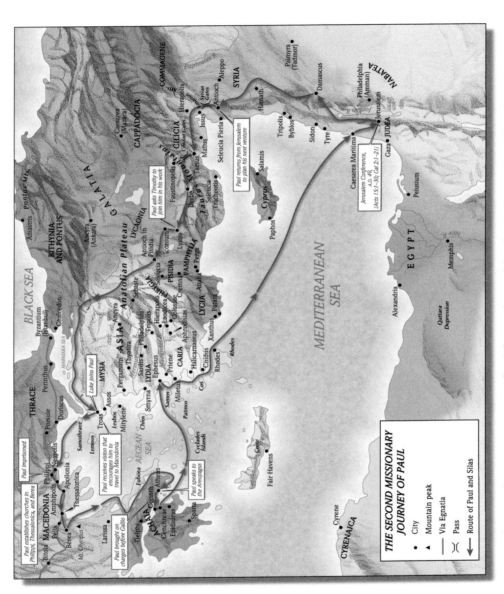

The Second Missionary Journey of Paul from Holman Bible Atlas © 1998, Holman Bible Publishers. Used by permission.

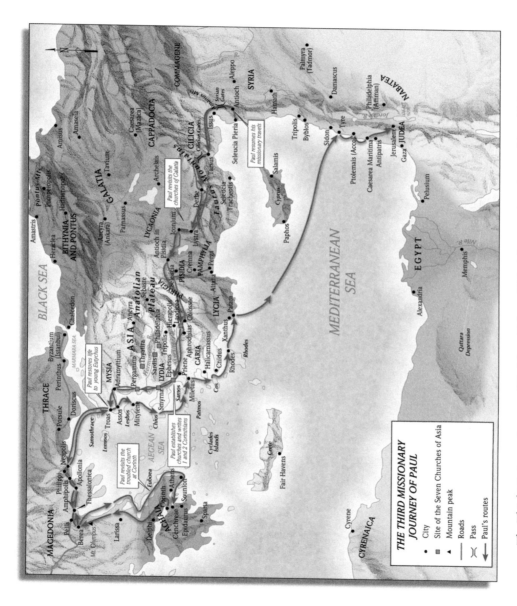

The Third Missionary Journey of Paul from Holman Bible Atlas © 1998, Holman Bible Publishers. Used by permission.

PAUL'S VOYAGE TO ROME

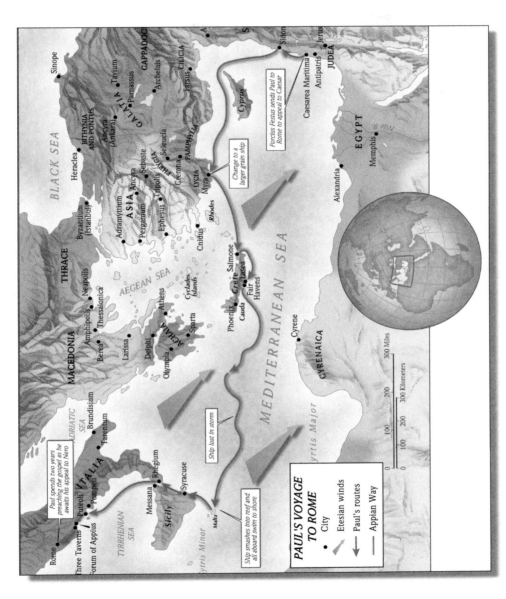

Paul's Voyage to Rome from Holman Bible Atlas © 1998, Holman Bible Publishers.
Used by permission.

ANSWER KEY TO OUTLINES

1 Timothy

I. Paul's Instruction Concerning Doctrine (1 Timothy 1)

   A. The GOAL of sound doctrine is:

      1. LOVE from a pure heart

      2. So one might keep a clean CONSCIENCE

      3. So believers will increase in a sincere FAITH

   B. Paul DEFENDED sound doctrine.

      1. Avoid LEGALISM.

      2. Avoid GNOSTICISM.

   C. Paul testified to God's GRACE.

   D. Paul instructed Timothy to "FIGHT THE GOOD FIGHT" (1 Timothy 1:18).

II. Paul's Instruction Concerning Public Worship (1 Timothy 2)

   A. PRAYER is the most essential part of public worship.

   B. Prayer includes:

      1. ENTREATIES (desires, needs)

      2. PRAYERS (bold access to God)

      3. PETITIONS (requests, intercessions)

      4. THANKSGIVING (giving thanks)

   C. Paul gave instruction for women in the church.

1. They must DRESS properly.

III. PAUL'S INSTRUCTION CONCERNING CHURCH LEADERS (1 TIMOTHY 3)

A. Paul listed the character traits of an ELDER (bishop).

1. His job is to oversee the SPIRITUAL life of the church.

2. He must be above REPROACH.

3. He must be tolerant, prudent, respectful, hospitable, and able to TEACH.

4. He must have a good REPUTATION outside of the church.

B. Paul listed the character traits of a DEACON.

1. The traits of a deacon are similar to that of an ELDER.

2. The deacon's job is to SERVE.

IV. PAUL'S INSTRUCTION CONCERNING FALSE TEACHERS (1 TIMOTHY 4)

A. Paul IDENTIFIED the false teachers.

B. He instructed Timothy to STAND firm against false teachers:

1. KNOW the Word of God.

2. DISCIPLINE yourself for godliness.

3. FIX your hope on the living God.

4. Read, teach, and EXHORT through the Word of God.

5. USE your spiritual gifts.

6. PERSEVERE in these things.

V. PAUL'S INSTRUCTION CONCERNING PASTORS' RELATIONSHIPS WITH CHURCH MEMBERS (1 TIMOTHY 5:1–6:5)

A. Treat all with RESPECT and honor them as family.

B. U<u>WIDOWS</u> have a special place in the church.

C. H<u>ONOR</u> godly elders and discipline those who continue in sin.

D. False teachers should be <u>IDENTIFIED</u>.

VI. PAUL'S INSTRUCTION CONCERNING TIMOTHY (1 TIMOTHY 6:6–21)

A. Flee from the love of <u>MONEY</u>.

B. <u>FIGHT</u> the good fight.

2 TIMOTHY

I. PAUL GAVE TIMOTHY THE CHARACTERISTICS OF "THE MAN OF GOD" (2 TIMOTHY 1–2).

A. Paul greeted Timothy as his beloved <u>SON</u> in the faith.

B. Paul <u>ENCOURAGED</u> Timothy with loving words.

C. Timothy was reminded of his <u>CALL</u> and of God's enabling power.

D. The qualifications of a <u>SOLDIER</u> of Christ were described.

E. Timothy was told how to be a <u>WORKER</u> pleasing to Christ.

II. PAUL GAVE TIMOTHY CAUTIONS FOR "THE MAN OF GOD" (2 TIMOTHY 3).

A. Know the <u>SIGNS</u> of the last days.

B. <u>ENDURE</u> suffering as Paul had done because:

1. The Lord was faithful to <u>DELIVER</u> him.

2. All who desire to live for Christ will be <u>PERSECUTED</u>.

3. <u>EVIL</u> men will go from bad to worse — deceiving and being deceived.

C. Timothy must <u>CONTINUE</u> in what he had learned and remember from whom and where he learned it.

D. All Scripture is "God breathed," or <u>INSPIRED</u>.

E. Scripture is valuable because:

    1. It teaches by explaining what's <u>RIGHT</u>.

    2. It reproves by explaining what's <u>WRONG</u>.

    3. It corrects by explaining how to <u>GET RIGHT</u>.

    4. It instructs by explaining how to <u>STAY RIGHT</u>.

    5. It completes and <u>EQUIPS</u> "the Man of God" for kingdom work.

III. PAUL CHALLENGED TIMOTHY WITH A CHARGE FOR "THE MAN OF GOD" (2 TIMOTHY 4).

    A. Timothy was charged to:

        1. <u>PREACH</u> the good news.

        2. Be <u>READY</u> at all times to instruct people.

        3. <u>REPROVE</u> those who are doing wrong.

        4. <u>REBUKE</u> sinners with stern reprimands.

        5. <u>ENCOURAGE</u> with great patience and careful teaching.

    B. A time would come when people would no longer listen to <u>TRUTH</u> but would desire teachers who would say what they wanted to hear.

    C. Paul's last letter to Timothy ends with very <u>PERSONAL</u> words.

TITUS

I. THE PROTECTION OF SOUND DOCTRINE IN THE CHURCH (TITUS 1)

    A. Paul instructed Titus to ordain qualified <u>LEADERS</u> in the church.

        1. <u>OVERSEERS</u> — bishops; had special responsibilities to superintend; pastors

        2. <u>ELDERS</u> — senators; older ones; appointed by apostles; had spiritual giftedness

        3. <u>DEACONS</u> — servants of someone; helpers; practical agents

B. Paul ordered Titus to choose leaders whose overall CHARACTER was blameless.

    1. DOMESTICALLY — with their wives and children at home

    2. PERSONALLY — respected in the community and at work

    3. DOCTRINALLY — know and show the Word

C. Paul encouraged Titus to rebuke the FALSE teachers in the church.

II. THE PRACTICE OF SOUND DOCTRINE IN THE CHURCH (TITUS 2)

A. Paul directed Titus to teach the older men and women to MENTOR the younger men and women.

    1. TRAIN — to advise; to instruct; suggests a close relationship between elder and younger

    2. ENCOURAGE — to give hope; to urge on; to help develop; to exhort

    3. EXAMPLE — to give a visible impression; to illustrate; to show quality or characteristics

    4. TEACH — to give verbal instruction; to impart knowledge or information

    5. REBUKE — to reprove sharply; to correct; to bring to light; to expose wrong

B. Paul insisted that Titus train the younger men and women to be SELF-CONTROLLED.

C. Paul told Titus to teach slaves to be OBEDIENT and trustworthy.

III. THE PARTICIPATION IN SOUND DOCTRINE IN THE WORLD (TITUS 3)

A. Paul required all members to OBEY the law of the land.

B. Paul reminded the believers why they should do profitable, GOOD works.

C. Paul demanded that the congregation avoid UNPROFITABLE and useless works.

PHILEMON

SEVEN REASONS TO BELIEVE THE BIBLE:

1. UNITY: The sixty-six books were written by forty authors over 1,500 years, but they tell one unified story.

2. CLAIMS: The Bible claims to be God's Word written by men moved by the Spirit.

3. HISTORY: Tests of archaeology and bibliography have never refuted it.

4. PROPHECY: Prophecy of the Bible has been fulfilled.

5. SURVIVAL: Man's many attempts to destroy it have failed (see Mark 13:31).

6. INFLUENCE: The Bible's influence on society has been more positive than any other book.

7. TRANSFORMATION: Individual lives have been transformed by it.

I. PHILEMON'S CHARACTER PRAISED (PHILEMON 1-7)

A. Philemon was Paul's beloved BROTHER and fellow worker.

B. Philemon's CHURCH met in his house.

C. Philemon had great faith toward God and LOVE toward the saints.

II. PHILEMON'S CHARACTER TESTED (PHILEMON 8-20)

A. Paul appealed to Philemon on behalf of Philemon's SLAVE, Onesimus.

B. Onesimus became USELESS. He stole from Philemon and ran away.

C. In Christ, Onesimus became USEFUL. He ministered to Paul.

D. Paul appealed to Philemon to ACCEPT Onesimus as a brother in the Lord.

E. Paul offered to REPAY Onesimus's debt.

III. **Philemon's Character Trusted (Philemon 21-25)**

A. Paul was confident Philemon would be <u>OBEDIENT</u> and do more than asked.

B. Paul was confident Philemon's <u>PRAYERS</u> would free him from prison.

IV. **Lessons We Learn from Philemon**

A. We need to be <u>FORGIVEN</u>.

B. It is not enough to be forgiven; we must also <u>FORGIVE</u>.

C. Once forgiven, we must make <u>RESTITUTION</u>.

NOTES

1 TIMOTHY

1. Philo, cited in William Barclay, *The Letters to Timothy, Titus, and Philemon*, rev. ed. (Philadelphia: Westminster, 1975), p. 107.

2. Aristotle, cited in Barclay, p. 107.

3. Randy Alcorn, *Money, Possessions and Eternity* (Wheaton, Ill.: Tyndale, 1989), p. 69.

2 TIMOTHY

1. William Barclay, *The Letters to Timothy, Titus, and Philemon*, rev. ed. (Philadelphia: Westminster, 1975), p. 21.

2. Barclay, p. 21.

3. Dietrich Bonhoeffer, *Life Together* (San Francisco: HarperSanFrancisco, 1954), p. 77.

TITUS

1. Bill Thrall, Bruce McNicol, and Ken McElrath, *The Ascent of a Leader* (San Francisco: Jossey-Bass, 1999), pp. 1-2.

2. Philip Yancey, *What's So Amazing About Grace?* (Grand Rapids, Mich.: Zondervan, 1997), p. 45.

PHILEMON

1. William Barclay, *The Letters to Timothy, Titus, and Philemon*, rev. ed. (Philadelphia: Westminster, 1975), p. 270.

2. D. Edmond Hiebert, *An Introduction to the Pauline Epistles* (Chicago: Moody, 1954), p. 241.

3. W. Graham Scroggie, *Know Your Bible: A Brief Introduction to the Scriptures*, vol. 2, *The New Testament* (London: Pickering and Inglis, n.d.), p. 201.

4. James Emery White, *Life-Defining Moments* (Colorado Springs, Colo.: WaterBrook, 2001), p. 116.

5. A. Norman Jeffares and Martin Gray, eds., *A Dictionary of Quotations* (New York: Barnes and Noble, Inc., 1995), p. 519.

LEADER'S GUIDE

1. *Webster's New Collegiate Dictionary* (Springfield, Mass.: G&C Merriam Co. Publishers, 1960), p. 237.

2. John K. Brilhart, *Effective Group Discussion* (Dubuque, Iowa: Wm. C. Brown Company Publishers, 1967), p. 26.

3. *How to Lead Small Group Bible Studies* (Colorado Springs, Colo.: NavPress, 1982), pp. 40-42.

BIOGRAPHIES

PAT HARLEY
Teacher

Pat committed her life to Jesus Christ at the age of thirty-two after He powerfully intervened and healed her broken marriage. After eight years of study, she began teaching the Bible to women, convinced that it is the Word of God that offers help and hope for women today. She is the founder and president of Big Dream Ministries, Inc. and served for eighteen years as the director of The Women's Fellowship, a former ministry to over five hundred women. She also served as the director of women's ministries at Fellowship Bible Church in Roswell, Georgia. Pat has a master of arts degree in education from Western Michigan University and has taken courses at Dallas Theological Seminary. She and her husband have two married daughters and several grandchildren.

ELEANOR LEWIS
Teacher

At the age of twenty-six, Eleanor accepted Christ for assurance of heaven. However, when her son was born with a severe birth defect, she turned to God's Word for answers and found not only a Savior but an all-powerful Lord. The Word of God came alive for her, and she began teaching and speaking at Christian women's clubs. For almost thirty years, she has taught Bible studies in churches, homes, and offices. In addition, she speaks at conferences and retreats across the country and internationally. She is president of Insights and Beginnings, Inc., which produced a video series and Bible study to help people understand their temperament types, overcome weaknesses, and use their strengths for the glory of God. Eleanor and her husband live in the Atlanta area and have a married son and one grandchild.

MARGIE RUETHER
Teacher

Though Margie was not raised in a churchgoing home, her parents committed their lives to Christ after Margie was in college. It was her mother's godly example and prayers that brought Margie to the throne of grace. Her growing love for Jesus and His Word led her to Bible Study Fellowship International, an interdenominational Christian organization in which laypeople teach Bible studies. After many years of study, she became a Substitute Teaching Leader and a member of the area team. She served there for a number of years before becoming one of the lead teachers at The Women's Fellowship in Roswell, Georgia. She has also facilitated a Bible teacher-training program for women and speaks at retreats and church conferences. She and her family live in Delaware.

LINDA SWEENEY
Teacher

Linda accepted Christ as her personal Savior when she was twelve years old. As an adult, she grew to love God's Word more and more. She began to see God change not only her life but the lives of others when they adhere to the wisdom of Scripture. Because of her passion to excite women to know the Word and to see their lives change as they respond in obedience, she began teaching the Bible to women in her church and community under God's leading. She has taught Sunday school for many years and was a much-loved Bible Study Fellowship International Teaching Leader for eight years. During that time, she not only taught hundreds of women weekly but also trained a large group of Bible Study Fellowship International leaders in her class. She has taught women's retreats and spoken at women's meetings and conferences throughout the South. She and her husband live in the Atlanta area and have a married daughter, a son, and two grandchildren.

ART VANDER VEEN
Senior Copywriter

Art began his relationship with Christ at age thirteen. In his late twenties after graduating from the University of New Mexico, he began preparing for full-time ministry. He earned a Th.M. degree from Dallas Theological Seminary and has ministered on the staff of Campus Crusade for Christ. He was one of the original team members of Walk Thru the Bible Ministries and served as chaplain for the Atlanta Falcons. In 1979, he was part of a team that founded Fellowship Bible Church in Roswell, Georgia, where he was a pastor for nearly twenty-five years. He now serves as pastor, teacher, and mentor at Little Branch Community Church in the Atlanta area. Art is passionate about helping people understand the Scriptures as the revealed truth from and about God. He and his wife, Jan, have three married children and seven grandchildren.

CARRIE OTT
Editor, Designer

Carrie met Christ at an early age. All her life she has had a passion for words, and as a freelance writer and designer, this passion doubles when it is words — seen, read, and grasped — that attempt to sketch a portrait of the mystery and wonder of God and His Word. Carrie identifies with Mechtild of Magdeburg, who said, "Of the heavenly things God has shown me, I can speak but a little word, no more than a honeybee can carry away on its foot from an overflowing jar." Carrie and her husband have three children and live in the Atlanta area.

To learn more about
Big Dream Ministries, Inc. and
The Amazing Collection,
visit their website at:

www.theamazingcollection.org

LEADER'S GUIDE

INTRODUCTION

Leading a group Bible study can be a challenging but incredibly rewarding experience. This Leader's Guide will provide help with the "challenging" part, as you trust God to produce the "incredibly rewarding" piece.

This guide is not designed to take you step-by-step through the individual studies. Instead, it will offer some general guidance and instruction in principles and techniques. Most of what you learn here will not be specific to *The Amazing Collection* but applicable to many kinds of group study. The one exception is Appendix B.

Each section of this Leader's Guide will deal with a single subject, making it easier for you to return to the guide for future help and reference.

Thank you for accepting the challenge and responsibility of leading your group! We pray God will make this a rewarding and profitable experience for you.

DISCUSSION: THE ESSENTIAL COMPONENT

The words *small-group Bible study* are almost synonymous with the term *discussion*. While there are very significant places and purposes for lecturing (one-way communication), for the most part a small group is not one of them. Therefore, discussion is an essential component of a successful small-group experience.

Discussion is the investigation of a subject or question by two or more people using verbal dialogue. Webster defines it as "consideration of a question in open debate; argument for the sake of arriving at truth or clearing up difficulties." Additionally, the word *discuss* and its synonyms mean "to discourse about so as to reach conclusions or to convince. Discuss also implies a sifting or examining, especially by presenting considerations pro and con."[1]

Small-group Bible studies will not always include debate or argument, but there *should* always be investigation, examination, and the reaching of at least tentative conclusions.

There are many benefits to discussion-style learning compared to lectures or even to interaction that is dominated by one person. Discussion:

- Keeps every member more involved in the learning process
- Allows for self-disclosure, enabling the participants to get to know each other better
- Helps crystallize the thinking of each group member by creating a venue in which topics can be investigated at deeper levels
- Creates a more informal atmosphere, which encourages a sense of relaxed learning
- Provides the potential of uncovering misconceptions and correcting misinformation
- Fosters more permanent learning and change because people tend to better remember what is said rather than what is thought
- Builds a sense of community as participants cooperate in their search for truth and understanding

While small-group Bible studies that foster healthy discussion will realize the above benefits, the depth of any group experience is greatly enhanced by an able leader. The leader plays an important role in helping each of these seven benefits become reality. For example, in order to keep every member more involved in the learning process, the leader will need to encourage those who tend to hide and manage those who tend to dominate. The other benefits require similar sensitivity by the leader. The remainder of this guide is intended to help the leader maximize these benefits for the small group.

But before we move on, one more issue should be addressed. While the leader is a crucial player in a small group, he or she should not become the person to whom all other participants address their remarks. One author has suggested that a discussion leader should strive to foster an "all-channel" network, rather than become the "hub" or center of a discussion wheel, as the following diagrams depict.

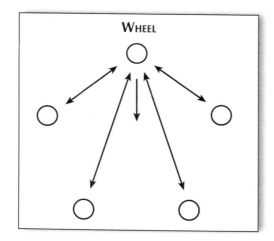

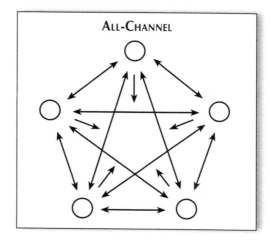

In a "wheel" network, all comments are directed toward one central leader, and he or she alone speaks to the group as a whole or to any one person.

By contrast, an "all-channel" network allows rapid communication without requiring clearance from a central gatekeeper; everyone is free to share thoughts that come to mind while they are still relevant to the topic at hand. Free exchange of questions and responses is thus encouraged.[2]

The leader's responsibility is to continually remember the need for "all-channel" communication.

LISTENING: THE LOST ART

You've probably heard it said that God gave us two ears and one mouth because He wanted us to listen twice as much as we talk. It would be difficult to prove that assumption, but the Bible *does* say:

> But everyone must be quick to hear, slow to speak. (James 1:19)

> He who gives an answer before he hears,
> It is folly and shame to him. (Proverbs 18:13)

Listening may be the most powerful tool of a successful small-group leader, but it is also possibly the most difficult trait to develop. Most people tend to talk more than listen, be more concerned about their interests than the interests of others, and listen impatiently, hoping the other person will finish quickly. True listening is a lost art, which a good small-group leader must recapture.

Listening is not just hearing. As reading is to seeing, listening is to hearing. By both reading and listening, we understand the real meaning of the words our senses "take in."

Consider the following ideas and use them to evaluate your own listening habits and skills. Then, decide which areas you could intentionally improve.

Listening Characteristics:
- It is active, not passive, and therefore sometimes tiring.

- It is other-centered, not self-centered, and therefore sometimes sacrificial.

- It is crucial, not peripheral, and therefore indispensable.

- It is difficult, not easy, and therefore often neglected.

- It is scarce, not common, and therefore greatly desirable.

Listening is not like:

- A chess game — planning your next verbal move while the other person is talking

- A trial — judging what is said or how it is said

- A 100-yard dash — thinking how quickly you can end the discussion

Listening is like:

- A sponge — absorbing as much as possible of what is being said and the feelings behind it

- A pair of binoculars — fixing attention on and bringing into clear focus what is being said

Kinds of Questions:

- Information — "What did you do today?"

- Opinion — "Why do you think that happened?"

- Feeling — "How do you feel about that?"

Kinds of Responses:

- Clarification — "I think what you're saying is . . ." This gets at the meaning of what was said.

- Observation — "I noticed that your voice dropped when . . ." This acknowledges the importance of nonverbal cues.

- Reflection — "You seem quite sad about . . ." This acknowledges the emotional component.

- Inquiry — "Tell me more about . . ." This seeks additional information and often gleans further insight.

While you are listening, consider silently praying for wisdom:

- "God, what are you doing in this person's heart right now?"

- "Father, help me to hear what she is really saying."

- "Eternal Counselor, what kind of response do you want me to make to what this person is saying?"

There will be times as a small-group leader when you will need to limit one member's input to allow for total group input. Your aim is not to encourage never-ending dialogue with one person, but to bring the most and the best out of each participant and the group as a whole, maximizing discussion, insight, and impact more fully than you may have thought possible.

Questions: The Mental Crowbars

Good questions can spell the difference between success and failure in a small-group setting. As you lead discussions of *The Amazing Collection*, the Learning for Life discussion questions at the beginning of each study will give you an excellent starting point. But there will be times when you will want to probe differently or more deeply. At such times, forming good questions will be incredibly important.

Some of these questions may be prepared ahead of time. Others will be developed as you go. Remember, every good question shares some common characteristics:

- Brief — short and uncluttered
- Applicable — relevant to the people's needs
- Simple — easily understood
- Interesting — capable of holding attention
- Conforming — based on the material being studied

As a leader you may ask launching, guiding, and application questions. The following material describes these three types of questions, giving examples of each.

Launching Questions:

- Initiate meaningful discussion on a subject
- May be prepared ahead of time
- Will determine to a large extent the direction your discussion will take
- Are general questions intended to stimulate discussion
- Must be based on the participants' previous study to enable quality contributions

  Examples:

  - "What did you discover in this passage about . . . ?"
  - "What impressed you most about how God . . . ?"
  - "What thoughts do you have about Moses after this study?"
  - "Why do you think God included this passage in the Bible?"
  - "How would you describe the holiness of God?"

Guiding Questions:

- Keep the discussion moving, drawing out the most important ideas and refocusing a wandering discussion
- May be prepared ahead of time as you anticipate the subjects that will be raised by the group

- May be crafted as the discussion is in high gear (This takes practice!)
- Take the participants beyond initial observations and more deeply into the meaning of the material

  Examples:
  - "Sally just mentioned the concept of obedience. How does that fit with what this passage seems to say?"
  - "Who else would like to comment on that?"
  - "We've said a lot of things about grace in our discussion. If you had to boil it down to a sentence, what would you say?"
  - "What we're discussing is interesting, but we've wandered from where we want to go. Can someone take us back to where we veered off the trail?"

Application Questions:
- Are supplied for you in *The Amazing Collection* workbooks
- May be developed based on your own knowledge of the group
- May be difficult to formulate but serve as the bridge from Bible study to daily living — from the head to the heart
- Do not always involve something concrete to do or to change
- Could include meditation, reflection, remembering, or simply waiting on God
- May be questions that will encourage the group to share their answers aloud or may suggest a more private response
- May be specific or general
- Must relate to the truth the group has just studied

  Examples:
  - "Write a prayer pouring out your heart to God in response to what He has been teaching you this week."
  - "Do you know someone who models well what we have just studied? How could you affirm that person this week?"
  - "What do you sense God is asking you to do in response to your study?"
  - "What do you see in this character's life that you would like to imitate? What would that look like? What is the first step?"

Crafting and asking questions are skills that can be developed and honed. After each group meeting, it might be useful to evaluate your questions. Did they lead the group where you sensed God wanted to lead? Which "as you go" guiding questions worked well or not so well? How did the group respond to the questions? Was there any confusion? Finally, make a point to review anything you learned about asking questions each week.

ROLES PEOPLE PLAY: THE ULTIMATE CHALLENGE

If being a small-group Bible study leader involved only facilitating discussion, learning to listen well, and forging meaningful questions, the challenge would be large enough. But add to that the fact that every person in your group will have different needs, temperaments and personalities, approaches to Bible study, reasons for being there, and levels of maturity, and the role of leadership becomes exponentially more challenging.

Professor Howard Hendricks of Dallas Theological Seminary describes in *How to Lead Small Group Bible Studies* some of the roles people play in group situations. You may find these helpful in evaluating your own group's dynamic.

Immature roles

The onlooker	Content to be a silent spectator. Only nods, smiles, and frowns. Other than this, he is a passenger instead of a crew member.
The monopolizer	Brother Chatty. Rambles roughshod over the rest of the conversation with his verbal dexterity. Tenaciously clings to his right to say what he thinks — even without thinking.
The belittler	This is Mr. Gloom. He minimizes the contributions of others. Usually has three good reasons why some opinion is wrong.
The wisecrack	Feels called to a ministry of humor. Mr. Cheerio spends his time as the group playboy. Indifferent to the subject at hand, he is always ready with a clever remark.
The hitchhiker	Never had an original thought in his life. Unwilling to commit himself. Sits on the sidelines until others reach a conclusion, then jumps on the bandwagon.
The pleader	Chronically afflicted with obsessions. Always pleading for some cause or action. Feels led to share this burden frequently. One-track mind.
The sulker	Lives with a resentful mood. The group won't always agree entirely with his views, so he sulks.

Mature roles

The proposer	Initiates ideas and action. Keeps things moving.
The encourager	Brings others into the discussion. Encourages others to contribute. Emphasizes the value of their suggestions and comments. Stimulates others to greater activity by approval and recognition.

The clarifier	Has the ability to step in when confusion, chaos, and conflict occur. He defines the problem concisely. Points out the issues clearly.
The analyzer	Examines the issues closely. Weighs suggestions carefully. Never accepts anything without first thinking it through.
The explorer	Always moving into new and different areas. Probes relentlessly. Never satisfied with the obvious or the traditional viewpoints.
The mediator	Promotes harmony between members — especially those who have trouble agreeing. Seeks to find conclusions acceptable to all.
The synthesizer	Able to put the pieces together from different ideas and viewpoints.[3]

No doubt you will see some of these roles typified by members of your small group. How you deal with members who play out the immature roles and how you encourage and utilize those who take on the mature ones will be an ongoing challenge. Ask the Spirit of God to give you sensitivity, creativity, and ability as you lead. Pray for wisdom to become your constant, ready resource.

Your Leadership: A Spiritual Endeavor

Before we move on, it is important to remember that beyond understanding and fostering discussion, learning to listen well, developing your skill in fashioning questions, and learning to lead different kinds of people, it is God who supplies the grace and strength that will carry you through the challenges of leadership.

This Leader's Guide has focused so far on you and your best efforts, but in truth you will accomplish absolutely nothing of eternal value unless the Spirit of God takes your faithful efforts and infuses them with His enabling power and grace.

For this reason, we encourage you to prepare and lead in complete humility, dependence, and trust, remembering these critical precepts:

I can do all things through Him who strengthens me. (Philippians 4:13)

"My grace is sufficient for you, for power is perfected in weakness." (2 Corinthians 12:9)

"I am the vine, you are the branches; he who abides in Me and I in him, he bears much fruit, for apart from Me you can do nothing." (John 15:5)

Finally, be strong in the Lord and in the strength of His might. Put on the full armor of God, so that you will be able to stand firm against the schemes of the devil. (Ephesians 6:10-11)

Our prayer for you is that of Paul's prayers for the Ephesians:

That the God of our Lord Jesus Christ, the Father of glory, may give to you a spirit of wisdom and of revelation in the knowledge of Him. I pray that the eyes of your heart may be enlightened, so that you will know what is the hope of His calling, what are the riches of the glory of His inheritance in the saints, and what is the surpassing greatness of His power toward us who believe. These are in accordance with the working of the strength of His might. . . . [And] that He would grant you, according to the riches of His glory, to be strengthened with power through His Spirit in the inner man, so that Christ may dwell in your hearts through faith; and that you, being rooted and grounded in love, may be able to comprehend with all the saints what is the breadth and length and height and depth, and to know the love of Christ which surpasses knowledge, that you may be filled up to all the fullness of God. Now to Him who is able to do far more abundantly beyond all that we ask or think, according to the power that works within us, to Him be the glory in the church and in Christ Jesus to all generations forever and ever. Amen. (Ephesians 1:17-19; 3:16-21)

APPENDIX A

THE EFFECTIVE DISCUSSION LEADER: A WORTHY GOAL

This section presents a model for the effective discussion leader (EDL). You may not demonstrate every characteristic listed, nor do you need to. Some of these things you will do very well; others you will do okay; still others may be a weak area for you. That is just fine. Consider this list simply an ideal to aim for. Our hope is that it will motivate you to grow as a small-group leader by revealing your areas of strength and highlighting your areas of weakness for which you may need help. God never said He could use only perfect people in ministry. In fact, your limitations in one or more of these areas may allow for others in the group to come alongside and complement you by contributing their strengths.

You may choose to use this list with a group of leaders to discuss your common ministries and responsibilities and share with each other challenges and successes you've experienced as leaders. Hearing others' thoughts about each of these characteristics might encourage you as you continue to grow.

What key characteristics make an effective discussion leader?

1. EDLs have a good grasp of the material to be discussed.
   - They have studied the material in advance.
   - They have a clear purpose for the meeting.
   - They have an introduction planned.
   - They have questions planned.
   - They have a tentative conclusion in mind.
   - They have examined their own life in relation to the truth of the study.
   - They seek to be diligent workers who accurately handle the word of truth (see 2 Timothy 2:15).

2. EDLs are skilled in organizing group thinking.
   - They know how to use questions.

- They can detect tangents and gently but firmly bring the discussion back on track.

3. EDLs are open-minded.
   - They express judgments in a conditional way.
   - They encourage consideration of all points of view.
   - They encourage open-mindedness on the part of all the members.
   - They are able to handle incorrect answers by inviting further questioning or discussion.

4. EDLs are active participants.
   - They talk frequently yet not excessively.
   - They are not defensive or sensitive to disagreement or criticism.

5. EDLs are facilitators.
   - They do not give dictatorial directions.
   - They encourage participation by all.
   - They encourage interaction among all members.
   - They are able to manage members who tend to dominate discussion.
   - They are able to stimulate and involve shy or reticent members in nonthreatening ways.

6. EDLs speak well.
   - They speak clearly.
   - They speak in a concise, pertinent way.
   - They are not tactless, chattering, offensive speakers.

7. EDLs have respect for and sensitivity to others.
   - They are empathetic.
   - They do not attack others.
   - They do not cause others to "lose face."
   - They are aware of how others are reacting.
   - They are patient.

8. EDLs are self-controlled.
   - They can remain impartial when necessary.

- They can express their feelings in a direct, yet nonaccusatory manner.

9. EDLs can assume different roles.
   - They can give encouragement.
   - They can give direction when necessary.
   - They can insert humor to break the tension when appropriate.
   - They can lead the group in prayer to seek wisdom.
   - They can give personal attention to needy members.

10. EDLs give credit to the group and its members.
    - They praise the group for insights and progress.
    - They stress teamwork.
    - They make all the members feel important.
    - They value others as their equals.
    - They "do nothing from selfishness or empty conceit" but regard others as more important than themselves (Philippians 2:3).

11. EDLs are authentically transparent.
    - They share personal illustrations.
    - They share personal weaknesses, frustrations, pressures, and failures without seeking undue personal attention.
    - They share personal feelings.
    - They share personal requests.
    - They plan ahead so all this can be done with taste and genuineness.

12. EDLs are enthusiastic.
    - They pour themselves into the subject and the discussion of it.
    - They allow the subject to be poured into them by God prior to the discussion.
    - They recognize that genuine enthusiasm is a powerful motivator for others.

13. EDLs are properly critical and evaluative of their leadership.
    - They constantly look for ways to improve.
    - They regularly seek feedback and advice.
    - They consistently evaluate the various aspects of their leadership role.

- They remember that evaluation is not comparing themselves with others but is seeking the Holy Spirit's input on possible improvement.

14. EDLs know that leadership is a spiritual endeavor.

   - They regularly admit to God that apart from Him they can do nothing (see John 15:5).

   - They confidently say "I can do all things" and then humbly add "through Him who strengthens me" (Philippians 4:13).

   - They never forget God's promise that "My grace is sufficient for you" (2 Corinthians 12:9).

APPENDIX B

SUGGESTED FORMATS FOR *THE AMAZING COLLECTION*

The Amazing Collection is intentionally flexible to accommodate a variety of teaching settings and calendars. It is possible to complete the study of all sixty-six books of the Bible in two years by teaching a book a week for thirty-three weeks each year (excluding summers and holidays).

Another option would be to go through the material in three years, teaching a book a week for twenty-two weeks each year, perhaps beginning in September and going through April. Also, for individuals, the program could be completed in approximately fifteen months, studying a book a week for sixty-six consecutive weeks.

There is flexibility in each individual session as well. Sessions might last an hour, in which the group watches the video (forty-five minutes) and allows fifteen minutes for discussion. Or, a 1.5-hour format could include the video, fifteen minutes for refreshments, fifteen for discussion, and fifteen for homework review. If time permits, two-hour sessions could include the video, refreshments, thirty minutes for discussion, and thirty for homework review.

Maybe you'll discover another format that suits your group to a tee. Feel free to use it!

APPENDIX C

SHARING THE GOSPEL

Leaders should be sensitive to the fact that some group members may have an interest in the Bible without having established a personal relationship with its central figure, Jesus Christ.

Sharing the gospel is quite easy for some people and more challenging for others. But if you sense that there are members in your group who would benefit from a clear explanation of salvation, by all means, offer one! There may even be "natural" openings during your course of study (at the end of a book or workbook or during your study of the Gospels or the book of Romans) when the gospel seems to "tell itself." In addition, the vast majority of discussion questions (Old and New Testament) contain a question that points directly to the person of Jesus Christ. These are "teachable moments." Don't miss them.

Several excellent tools exist that can help you walk an unbeliever through the basics of salvation. *The Four Spiritual Laws*, *Steps to Peace with God*, *My Heart — Christ's Home*, and *The Roman Road* are just a few. The leaders in your church may be able to provide you with one or more of them.

Although there are many excellent video testimonies throughout *The Amazing Collection*, it may be appropriate at some point to briefly share your own personal testimony with your group or with one or more of its members. It may help to think of your "story" in four parts: your life before Christ, how you came to know and understand your need for forgiveness and reconciliation with God, what Christ did on your behalf on the cross, and how your life is different today having accepted His atoning sacrifice on your behalf. This is your story! Pray for a sensitive heart, the right timing, and the right words to share it when the Holy Spirit leads you to do so.

It is our prayer that no one would complete *The Amazing Collection* without a personal, saving knowledge of our Savior, the Lord Jesus Christ.